D0130218

Traverse Theatre Company

Damascus

by David Greig

cast in order of appearance

Elena	Dolya Gavanski
Paul	Paul Higgins
Zakaria	Khalid Laith
Muna	Nathalie Armin
Wasim	Alex Elliott

Director	Philip Howard
Designer	Anthony MacIlwaine
Lighting Designer	Chahine Yavroyan
Composer & Arranger	Jon Beales
Sound Designer	Graham Sutherland
Dialect Coach	Ros Steen
Assistant Director	David Overend

Stage Manager	Gemma Smith
Deputy Stage Manager	Natasha Lee-Walsh
Assistant Stage Manager	Sarah Holland
Wardrobe Supervisor	Aileen Sherry

**first performed at the Traverse Theatre,
Friday 27 July 2007**

a Traverse Theatre Commission

THE TRAVERSE

Artistic Director Philip Howard

A Rolls-Royce machine for promoting new Scottish drama across Europe and beyond.
(The Scotsman)

The Traverse's commissioning process embraces a spirit of innovation and risk-taking that has launched the careers of many of Scotland's best-known writers including John Byrne, David Greig, David Harrower and Liz Lochhead. It is unique in Scotland in that it fulfils the crucial role of providing the infrastructure, professional support and expertise to ensure the development of a dynamic theatre culture for Scotland.

The importance of the Traverse is difficult to overestimate . . . without the theatre, it is difficult to imagine Scottish playwriting at all. (Sunday Times)

From its conception in the 1960s, the Traverse has remained a pivotal venue during the Edinburgh Festival. It receives enormous critical and audience acclaim for its programming, as well as regularly winning awards. From 2001–05, Traverse Theatre productions of *Gagarin Way* by Gregory Burke, *Outlying Islands* by David Greig, *Iron* by Rona Munro, *The People Next Door* by Henry Adam, *Shimmer* by Linda McLean, *When the Bulbul Stopped Singing* by Raja Shehadeh and *East Coast Chicken Supper* by Martin J Taylor have won Fringe First or Herald Angel Awards (and occasionally both).

2006 was a record-breaking year for the Traverse as their Festival programme *Passion* picked up an incredible 14 awards including a Herald Angel Award for their own production of *Strawberries in January* by Evelyne de la Chenelière in a version by Rona Munro.

The Traverse Theatre has established itself as Scotland's leading exponent of new writing, with a reputation that extends worldwide. (The Scotsman)

The Traverse's success isn't limited to the Edinburgh stage, since 2001 Traverse productions of *Gagarin Way, Outlying Islands, Iron, The People Next Door, When the Bulbul Stopped Singing, The Slab Boys Trilogy, Mr Placebo* and *Helmet* have toured not only within Scotland and the UK, but in Sweden, Norway, the Balkans, Germany, USA, Iran, Jordan and Canada. Immediately following the 2006 festival, the Traverse's production of *Petrol Jesus Nightmare #5 (In the Time of the Messiah)* by Henry Adam was invited to perform at the International Festival in Priština, Kosovo and won the Jury Special Award for Production.

One of Europe's most important homes for new plays.
(Sunday Herald)

Now in its 14th year, the Traverse's annual Highlands & Islands tour is a crucial strand of their work. This commitment to Scottish touring has taken plays from their Edinburgh home to audiences all over Scotland. The Traverse has criss-crossed the nation performing at diverse locations from Shetland to Dumfries, Aberdeen to Benbecula. The Traverse's 2005 production *I was a Beautiful Day* was commissioned to open the new An Lanntair Arts Centre in Stornoway, Isle of Lewis.

Auld Reekie's most important theatre. (The Times)

The Traverse's work with young people is of supreme importance and takes the form of encouraging playwriting through its flagship education project *Class Act*, as well as the Young Writers' Group. *Class Act* is now in its 17th year and gives pupils the opportunity to develop their plays with professional playwrights and work with directors and actors to see the finished piece performed on stage at the Traverse. This year, for the fourth year running, the project also took place in Russia. In 2004 *Articulate*, a large scale project based on the *Class Act* model, took place in West Dunbartonshire working with 11 to 14-year-olds. The hugely successful Young Writers' Group is open to new writers aged between 18 and 25 and the fortnightly meetings are led by a professional playwright.

The Traverse has an unrivalled reputation for producing contemporary theatre of the highest quality, invention and energy, and for its dedication to new writing. (Scotland on Sunday)

The Traverse is committed to working with international playwrights and, in 2005, produced *In the Bag* by Wang Xiaoli in a version by Ronan O'Donnell, the first-ever full production of a contemporary Chinese play in the UK. This project was part of the successful Playwrights in Partnership scheme, which unites international and Scottish writers, and brings the most dynamic new global voices to the Edinburgh stage. Other international Traverse partnerships have included work in Québec, Norway, Finland, France, Italy, Portugal and Japan.

www.traverse.co.uk

To find out about ways in which you can support the work of the Traverse please contact our Development Department
0131 228 3223 or development@traverse.co.uk

Charity No. SC002368

COMPANY BIOGRAPHIES

Nathalie Armin (Muna)
Nathalie trained at the Central School of Speech & Drama, London. Theatre credits include *References to Salvador Dali* (Arcola Theatre); *Othello* (Royal Shakespeare Company); *Crazy Black Muthaf**kin' Self, Local* (Royal Court); *A Day Like Today* (Young Vic); *Shameless* (Birmingham Rep/ Soho Theatre); *My Dad's Corner Shop* (Birmingham Rep); *St Pancras Project* (Lift Festival); *Objects of Desire* (Soho Theatre). Television work includes *Spooks, Holby City, Eastenders, Casualty, Living It, William & Mary* (BBC); *Randall & Hopkirk Deceased* (Working Title); *The English Harem, The Bill* (ITV); *The Jury* (Granada). Radio work includes *Poppyseeds, Sugar and Snow, The Glad House, Keep on Running, Psyche* (BBC Radio 4). Film credits include *The Allotment, Grow Your Own* (BBC Films).

Jon Beales (Composer/Arranger)
Jon works extensively in theatre as a composer, musical director and sound designer. For the Traverse: *Gorgeous Avatar, Wormwood, The Speculator* (Grec Festival, Barcelona/Edinburgh International Festival), *Solemn Mass for a Full Moon in Summer* (Traverse/Barbican). Other theatre credits include *Flora the Red Menace, Sunshine on Leith* (Dundee Rep); *Laurel & Hardy, A Christmas Carol, Guys & Dolls, Mother Courage* (Royal Lyceum Theatre, Edinburgh); *Into The Woods, The Secret Garden, Honk!, Masterclass* (Byre Theatre); *Kissing Angels* (National Youth Theatre); *The Tempest, Feelgood, Travesties, Mary Rose, Dear Brutus, A Midsummer Night's Dream* (Nottingham Playhouse); *Oliver!* (Perth Theatre); *Cat on a Hot Tin Roof* (Nottingham/Coventry/Edinburgh); *The Grapes of Wrath* (7:84); *The 39 Steps, Time and the Conways, Travels with my Aunt* (national tours). Film credits include *The Audition, The Total Eclipse of Sybil Price, I Got You, Deadbeat, Wasteland.*

Alex Elliott (Wasim)
Alex trained at the University of Manchester. Theatre credits include *Como Agua Para Chocolate* (Théâtre Sans Frontières); *Writing Wrong* (Customs House, South Shields); *Grace* (Quarantine); *Clockwork Orange, Edmond, Glengarry Glenross, Smirnova's Birthday, Tiger's Bride* (Northern Stage); *Homage to Catalonia* (Northern Stage/ T. Romea); *Out of Nothing, One Day 49* (Le Styx); *Pandora's Box* (Kneehigh). Film & Television credits include *Emmerdale, The Royal* (Yorkshire Granada Television); *Eastenders* (BBC); *Cold Lazarus* (Whistling Gypsy); *Wycliffe* (HTV); *Soldier Soldier* (Carlton TV).

Dolya Gavanski (Elena)
Dolya trained at the University of Cambridge and studied Piano, Performance & Acting in Moscow and London. Theatre credits include *Rock 'n' Roll* (Duke of York's Theatre); *Nirvana* (Riverside Studios); *Hippolytos* (Thiasos Theatre Company); *Troilus and Cressida, Twelfth Night* (Festival Budva Theatre City); *Serious Money, Trojan Women, Elektra* (Cambridge Arts Theatre); *Dark of the Moon* (Lyric Studio). Film & Television includes: *Andromache, The Secret Life of Mona Lisa, Uraditi Pravu Stvar, Nataša.*

David Greig (Writer)
For the Traverse: *When the Bulbul Stopped Singing, Outlying Islands, The Speculator, Danny 306+Me Forever, The Architect, Europe.* Other theatre includes: *Futurology* (Suspect Culture/ National Theatre of Scotland); *Gobbo* (National Theatre of Scotland); *The American Pilot, Victoria* (Royal Shakespeare Company); *Ramallah* (Royal Court); *San Diego* (Edinburgh International Festival/Tron Theatre); *8000m, Lament, Casanova, Candide 2000, One Way Street, Airport, Timeless, Mainstream* (Suspect Culture); *Pyrenees, The Cosmonaut's Last Message to the Woman He Once Loved in the Former Soviet Union* (Tron Theatre); *Caledonia Dreaming* (7:84 Theatre Company);*Yellow Moon, Dr Korcak's Example* (TAG Theatre Company). Translations and adaptations include: *The Bacchae* (Edinburgh International Festival/National Theatre of Scotland); *Caligua* (Donmar Warehouse); *Battle of Will* (National Theatre Studio). He has written a number of radio plays for BBC Radio and is currently working on a full-length feature film for Kudos. David is dramaturg for the National Theatre of Scotland.

Paul Higgins (Paul)
Theatre includes: *The Tempest* (Tron Theatre); *Black Watch* (National Theatre of Scotland); *Paul, An Enemy of The People, The Hare Trilogy* (Royal National Theatre); *The Cosmonaut's Last Message To The Woman He Once Loved in the Former Soviet Union* (Donmar Warehouse); *Macbeth, Conversations After A Burial* (Almeida Theatre); *Measure for Measure* (Royal Shakespeare Company); *The Golden Ass, A Midsummer Night's Dream* (Globe Theatre); *Night Songs, American Bagpipes, Conquest of the South Pole, A Wholly Healthy Glasgow* (Royal Court); *Buried Alive, The Maiden Stone* (Hampstead Theatre); *The Way of the World, The Odd Women, Romeo and Juliet, A View From The Bridge* (Royal Exchange); the *Slab Boys Trilogy* (Young Vic); *The Birthday Party* (Shared Experience). Television work includes *The Last Enemy, The Thick of it* (BBC); *Low Winter Sun* (Tiger Aspect/ Channel 4); *Tumbledown, A Very Peculiar Practice* (BBC); *Staying Alive* (LWT). Film credits include: *Red Road* (Sigma/ Zentropa); *Complicity* (Talisman); *Bedrooms & Hallways* (Pandora Films).

Philip Howard (Director)

Philip trained under Max Stafford-Clark at the Royal Court Theatre, London, on the Regional Theatre Young Director Scheme from 1988-1990. He was Associate Director at the Traverse from 1993-1996, and has been Artistic Director since 1996. Productions at the Traverse include 21 world premieres of plays by David Greig, David Harrower, Iain F MacLeod, Linda McLean, Henry Adam, Catherine Czerkawska, Catherine Grosvenor, Sue Glover, Iain Heggie, Jules Horne, Nicola McCartney, Ronan O'Donnell and the late Iain Crichton Smith. Fringe First awards for *Kill the Old Torture Their Young, Wiping My Mother's Arse* and *Outlying Islands*; Jury Special Award for Production of *Petrol Jesus Nightmare #5 (In the Time of the Messiah)* at InFest, National Theatre of Priština, Kosovo. Other productions at the Traverse include *Faith Healer* by Brian Friel, *The Trestle at Pope Lick Creek* by Naomi Wallace, *Cuttin' a Rug* by John Byrne, *When the Bulbul Stopped Singing* by Raja Shehadeh (also Fadjr International Festival, Tehran; Off-Broadway, New York; Amman, Jordan) and, as Co-Director, *Solemn Mass for a Full Moon in Summer* by Michel Tremblay (Traverse/Barbican). Productions elsewhere include *Words of Advice for Young People* by Ioanna Anderson (Rough Magic, Dublin), *The Speculator* by David Greig in Catalan (Grec Festival, Barcelona/Edinburgh International Festival), *Entertaining Mr Sloane* (Royal, Northampton) and *Something About Us* (Lyric Hammersmith Studio). Radio credits include *Being Norwegian* by David Greig, *The Gold Digger* by Iain F MacLeod (BBC Radio Scotland); *The Room* by Paul Brennen (BBC Radio 4).

Khalid Laith (Zakaria)

Khalid trained at the Central School of Speech and Drama. Recent Theatre includes *Leaving Home* (King's Head Theatre). Television credits include *The Bill* (ITV), *Saddam's Tribe, The Mark of Cain, The Hamburg Cell* (Channel 4); *Spooks, The Inspector Lynley Mysteries* (BBC).

Anthony MacIlwaine (Designer)

For the Traverse: *When the Bulbul Stopped Singing, Iron, 15 Seconds, Quartz.* Other theatre includes: *The Barber of Seville, The Seagull* (Bristol Old Vic); *Almost Nothing, At The Table* (Royal Court); *Cinderella* (Lyric Hammersmith); *One Minute* (Actors Touring Company); *Prayers for Sherkin* (Old Vic); *The Mikado* (Grange Park Opera); *Making The Most Noise Quietly* (Oxford Stage Company); *Wozzeck, From the House of the Dead* (Long Beach Opera, California); *Dark Ride* (Soho Rep, New York); *Beauty and The Beast* (Young Vic); *Grimm Tales* (Haymarket Theatre, Leicester); *Cheating Hearts, The Lovers, Agamemnon's Children, Euripides Trilogy, Aurelie My Sister* (Gate Theatre); *Les Misérables* (Pimlico Opera for HMP Wandsworth).

David Overend (Assistant Director)

David studied Theatre & Dramaturgy at the University of Glasgow and was Literary Assistant at the Traverse Theatre 2005-06, before training at RADA. Directing credits include *Petra* by David Greig (Measureless Liars/GilmorehillG12); *The Gyntish Self, The Tempest, Afraid of the Dark?* (Measureless Liars); *Salome* (RADA). Assistant directing credits include *Aalst* (National Theatre of Scotland/Victoria). From Autumn 2007 David will be working as a Director in Residence at the Arches Theatre for a practice-as-research PhD with the University of Glasgow.

Ros Steen (Dialect Coach)

Ros trained at RSAMD and has worked extensively in theatre, film and TV. For the Traverse: *Carthage Must Be Destroyed; strangers, babies*, the *Tilt* triple bill, *Gorgeous Avatar, Melody, I was a Beautiful Day, East Coast Chicken Supper, The Found Man, In the Bag, Shimmer, The Nest*, the *Slab Boys Trilogy, Dark Earth, Homers, Outlying Islands, The Ballad of Crazy Paola, The Trestle at Pope Lick Creek, Heritage* (2001 and 1998), *Among Unbroken Hearts, Shetland Saga, Solemn Mass For a Full Moon in Summer* (as co-director) *King of the Fields, Highland Shorts, Family, Kill the Old Torture Their Young, Chic Nerds, Greta, Lazybed, Knives in Hens, Passing Places, Bondagers, Road to Nirvana, Sharp Shorts, Marisol, Grace in America*. Recent theatre credits include *The Bevellers, Shadow of a Gunman, No Mean City, Whatever Happened To Baby Jane?, Mystery of the Rose Bouquet* (Citizens Theatre); *Sweet Bird of Youth, The Talented Mr, Ripley, The Graduate, A Lie of the Mind* (Dundee Rep); *Black Watch, Mancub, Miss Julie* (National Theatre of Scotland); *The Wonderful World of Dissocia* (Edinburgh International Festival/Drum Theatre Plymouth/Tron Theatre), *The Rise and Fall of Little Voice* (Visible Fictions); *Perfect Pie* (Stellar Quines), *The Small Things* (Paines Plough); *My Mother Said I Never Should* (West Yorkshire Playhouse). Film credits include *Greyfriars Bobby*, (Piccadilly Pictures); *Gregory's Two Girls* (Channel Four Films). Television credits include *Sea of Souls, Rockface, 2000 Acres of Skye, Monarch of the Glen, Hamish Macbeth* (BBC).

Graham Sutherland (Sound Designer)

Graham trained at Glasgow University and currently works as Head of Lighting and Sound for the Citizens Theatre, Glasgow alongside his work as a freelance sound & lighting designer. For the Traverse: *Petrol Jesus Nightmare #5 (In the Time of the Messiah)* (Edinburgh Fringe 2006/Kosovan Tour); *Outlying Islands* (Highland Tour Relight). Lighting & Sound design credits for theatre include: *Tom Fool* (Citizens Theatre); *Snuff* (The Arches/National Theatre of Scotland). Other

Sound Design includes: *The Rise and Fall of Little Voice* (Visible Fictions); *White Death* (Sweetscar), *Frozen* (Rapture Theatre); *Slope, Blind_Sight* (Untitled Projects); *Freefall* (7:84 Theatre Company); *Stacy* (Hush Productions). As a Lighting Designer, theatre credits include: *Home-Dundee* (National Theatre of Scotland); *Romeo and Juliet, Blood Wedding* (Citizens Theatre); *Arlecchino's Revenge, Good Sister Bad, Fergus Steps Out, Distant Suma* (Lung Ha's Theatre Company); *Voyager Princess* (Sense Scotland); *Dying For It, Haroun and the Sea of Stories, Our Town* (Scottish Youth Theatre); *Seeing Voices* (Solar Bear); *Our Town* (GilmorehillG12). Graham has also worked as a professional mentor in sound design for the University of Glasgow and as a project manager on various professional development projects with the National Theatre of Scotland.

Chahine Yavroyan (Lighting Designer)

Chahine trained at the Bristol Old Vic Theatre School. For the Traverse: *Strawberries in January, When the Bulbul Stopped Singing, Outlying Islands, 15 Seconds, Iron, Green Field, Gagarin Way, Wiping My Mother's Arse; King Of The Fields, The Speculator, Danny 306+Me (4 Ever), Perfect Days, Kill the Old Torture Their Young, Anna Weiss, Knives In Hens, The Architect, Shining Souls*. Other theatre includes *Elizabeth Gordon Quinn, Realism* (National Theatre of Scotland); *The Wonderful World of Dissocia* (Edinburgh International Festival/Tron Theatre/Drum Theatre, Plymouth and National Theatre of Scotland); *San Diego, The Cosmonaut's Last Message to the Woman He Once Loved in the Former Soviet Union* (Tron Theatre); *Mahabharata* (Sadler's Wells); *The Death of Klinghoffer* (Edinburgh International Festival); *Long Time Dead, After The End* (Paines Plough); *How To Live* (Bobby Baker); *Mirror For Princes* (BITE); *Marriage of Figaro* (Tara Arts). He has worked extensively in theatre, with companies and artists including: The Crucible; Royal Court; Nottingham Playhouse; Leicester Haymarket; Institute of Contemporary Arts; English National Opera; Lindsay Kemp; Rose English; Pip Simmons. Dance work with: Yolande Snaith Theatredance; Bock & Vincenzi; Jasmin Vardimon; Anatomy Performance Company; Naheed Saddiqui, X Factor. Site Specific work includes *Dreams of a Winter Tale* (Belsay Hall); *Deep End* (Marshall St. Baths Spa); *Elizabeth Garrat* (Anderson Hospital); *Sleeping Beauty* (St. Pancras Chambers). Fashion work includes shows for Givenchy; Chalayan; Clemens-Riberio; Ghost. Chahine is a longstanding People Show person.

The Traverse Theatre receives financial assistance from:

The Barcapel Foundation The Binks Trust,
The Calouste Gulbenkian Foundation,
The Canadian High Commission, The Craignish Trust,
The Cross Trust, The Cruden Foundation,
Gouvernement de Québec,
James Thom Howat Charitable Trust,
The Japan Foundation, The John Thaw Foundation,
The Lloyds TSB Foundation for Scotland,
The Misses Barrie Charitable Trust,
The Peggy Ramsay Foundation,
Ronald Duncan Literary Foundation,
Sky Youth Action Fund, Tay Charitable Trust,
The Thistle Trust, The Weatherall Foundation

For their continued generous support of Traverse productions, the Traverse thanks:

Habitat
Marks and Spencer, Princes Street
Camerabase

For their help on Damascus, the Traverse thanks:

The Davis Family; The Pier, 104 George St, Edinburgh;
Roger Baines; Catherine Mew

ARE YOU DEVOTED?

Our Devotees are:

**Stewart Binnie, Katie Bradford,
Adrienne Sinclair Chalmers, Adam Fowler,
Anne Gallacher, Keith Guy,
Helen Pitkethly, Michael Ridings**

The Traverse could not function without the generous support of our patrons. In March 2006 the Traverse Devotees was launched to offer a whole host of exclusive benefits to our loyal supporters.

Become a Traverse Devotee for £28 per month or £350 per annum and receive:

- A night at the theatre including six tickets, drinks and a backstage tour

- Your name inscribed on a brick in our wall

- Sponsorship of one of our brand new Traverse 2 seats

- Invitations to Devotees' events

- Your name featured on this page in Traverse Theatre Company scripts and a copy mailed to you

- Free hire of the Traverse Bar Café (subject to availability)

Bricks in our wall and seats in Traverse 2 are also available separately. Inscribed with a message of your choice, these make ideal and unusual gifts.

To join the Devotees or to discuss giving us your support in another way, please contact our Development Department on 0131 228 3223 / development@traverse.co.uk

TRAVERSE THEATRE – THE COMPANY

David Greig
Damascus

faber and faber

First published in 2007
by Faber and Faber Limited
3 Queen Square, London WC1N 3AU

Typeset by Country Setting, Kingsdown, Kent CT14 8ES
Printed in the UK by CPI Bookmarque, Croydon, CR0 4TD

A CIP record for this book
is available from the British Library

ISBN 978-0-571-23917-7

2 4 6 8 10 9 7 5 3 1

Author's Note

Damascus came about as an unexpected by-product of the artistic exchange I have been privileged to have with young theatre makers in the Middle East, particularly in Syria and Palestine, since 2000. During that time I have led a number of playwriting workshops in the region facilitated and encouraged by, amongst other organisations, the British Council. These workshops were aimed at introducing young Arab writers to the techniques of new British playwriting but – whatever the Arab writers learned – the workshops ended up teaching me an enormous amount about the complexities of relations between the West and the Arab world.

As well as the young writers, and their plays, I had other wonderful guides on my journey through this metaphorical and literal Damascus. Many people gave me the benefit of their time, their thoughts and their stories. Inevitably I have borrowed from these in my writing. While the characters and events of this play are wholly my own invention, I couldn't possibly have written this play without the generosity of a host of people in Damascus, Ramallah and Beit Jala. I would like say thank you to Leila, Nidal, Shaza, Nisreen, Abdullah, Ahmedia, Lama, Wael, Shaaden, Somar; to the writers and actors on the Damascus workshops of 2005–6; to the writers involved in the Damascus and Tunisia 2007 workshops; to the actors and writers at Al Kasaba, Ramallah, in 2000–1 and the actors and company at Inad Theatre, Beit Jala; to Raja and Penny Shehadeh in Ramallah; and to a multitude of other guides, talkers, teachers and walkers with me whose thoughts have contributed to and influenced this play.

David Greig, June 2007

Characters

Paul

Elena

Zakaria

Muna

Wasim

Setting

The play takes place in the foyer
of a small hotel in Damascus

A Note on the Language

Indented dialogue indicates that, even though
we hear the words in English, the character is,
in reality, speaking Arabic.

Paul does not understand Arabic. Paul's French
in the play is intended to be full of mistakes.
The Dean speaks better French.

*Language, you terrible surrounder
of everything*

W. S. Graham
Implements in Their Right Places

Act One

ONE

Dawn.
  The hotel foyer.
  In the foyer there are: a small reception desk with a postcard stand; an area with armchairs; a breakfast area with chairs and tables; a very small dance floor with a glitterball; and a small bar with drinks and snacks.
  Framed photographs of the President are hung behind the bar and the reception desk.
  Beside the dance floor there is a piano.
  On the breakfast tables are set small vases with jasmine flowers.
  A television plays in the bar with the sound down low.
  The television shows news images of the current situation.
    Elena sits at the piano and plays very sparse music.

Elena At this time of the morning I play the notes so far apart you might not even notice that it's music, but it is.

  She pours herself a drink.
  She pours a drink for you.

God, you look terrible.

Have you even slept?

Sit.

Drink.

You want to know what happened.

I know.

I was here in the beginning.

7

I was here at the end.

I'm always here.

Always.

My name is Elena.

Welcome to Damascus.

The call to prayer begins.

TWO

Soon, many mosques all over the city are issuing the call.
    The effect is of a Debussy chord rising, dissonant but comforting.
    Paul enters, pulling a wheelie suitcase behind him.
    He looks about him.

Paul Hello.
    Hello.

He rings the reception bell.

Paul takes out his mobile.
    He sits down in one of the foyer chairs.
    He makes a call on his mobile.

Hi, it's me . . . Yeah – I forgot to tell you something about the car. The passenger side wheel. It's making a noise. I thought it could be the wheel bearing . . . Could you listen out for it? . . . Just monitor it . . . It's a sort of –

He imitates the noise of a car with a faulty wheel-bearing.

No, it's perfectly safe . . . You sound stressed . . . You're not stressed . . . You sound stressed – are you sure you're not stressed? . . . If you're sure . . . Why don't you call my mother and she can look after the kids and –

OK.
    Bye.
    Love you.

He ends the call.

Something of a pause.

*He goes over to the a vase of jasmine flowers on a
table.*
    He smells the jasmine flowers.

He makes another call on the mobile.

It's me again – I think I might have lost my sense of smell.
I can't smell anything . . . I need a number for NHS
Direct –

On the plane –

A pie –

I don't know, some type of a – I suspect it was a chicken
pie . . . I would have expected it to have an aroma . . .
No – I tried the perfumes on the plane . . . Really
nothing. I've just tried a flower here . . . I don't know a –
a – jasmine?

What if it never comes back?

I know but what if . . . ? What if, though? What if?

Grass . . . the children's hair . . . incipient rain.

0-8-4-5-2-4-2-4-2-4. OK – you can go back to your bath
. . . Sorry – I know . . . I know . . . Love you.

    He ends the call.

Fuck. Piss. Cock.

    Beat.
        He returns to reception.
        He rings the bell.

Zakaria enters, holding a jasmine flower.
Zakaria looks at him.

I'm booked. I have a room.

Zakaria goes behind the reception desk.
He puts on a pair of white gloves.

Hartstone. Paul Hartstone.

Zakaria One moment.

Zakaria checks a ledger.

I am your reception.

Paul Right.

Zakaria Welcome.

Zakarias gets a booking form from a drawer.
He begins to fill out the check-in form.

Paul's mobile phone rings.
He answers.

Paul Hi, Sean . . . I only just got here. I haven't even checked into my room . . . There's nobody . . . No, I'm not watching porn – this is an Arabic . . . There's no porn . . . A Muslim country, Sean . . . Can we speak later?

Zakaria Passport.

Paul hands over his passport. Zakaria reads it.

Paul Not even in hotels . . . It's three o clock in the morning . . . No, Sean – I'm going to go in to make the deal and get out . . . This is supposed to be you, by the way – it's Valentine's Day, I should be at home . . . Why me? Why do I have to come to a war zone?

It is a war zone.

It's not ridiculous.

Iraq and Gaza – the Gaza thing, and Iran and . . .

No . . . Yes, exactly . . . No, no, because if I wanted to cause harm to – to terrorise, what would I do? I'll tell you – I'll tell you what I would do – I would stand amongst the glass and ivy in the lobby of a five-star hotel and spray bullets from my Kalashnikov into the businessmen and arms dealers and – and, yes! – sellers of educational textbooks.

It's not actually five-star.

Three-star.

Bye.

He ends the call.

Zakaria has finished filling out the form.

Thank you.
In the room, is there pay TV?

Zakaria Pay TV?

Paul You know – movies.

Zakaria No pay TV.

Paul Right.

Zakaria Room five hundred-six.

Paul Thank you.

Zakaria gives Paul a key.
He gives Paul back his passport.

Zakaria You are writer.

Paul Yes.

Zakaria Welcome.
I am Zakaria.

Zakaria climbs over the desk and takes Paul's suitcase.

I am your porter.
You are in Damascus before?

Paul No.

Zakaria You are welcome.

Paul Thank you.

Zakaria points out of the window.

Zakaria Here is Mount Quissoon.

Paul looks.

Paul I see.

Zakaria Abraham walks on this mountain.

Beat.

A house here is very expensive.

Paul Really?

Zakaria You are welcome.

Beat.

Where are you from?

Paul Scotland.

Zakaria Scotland.

Paul You know it?

Zakaria No.

Beat.

Paul Zakaria, this flower. What is it? Is it jasmine?

Zakaria Jasmine.

Paul Does it have a smell?

Zakaria This flower is plastic, Mr Paul.

Paul Thank you.

Zakaria leads Paul over to the lift.

He presses the lift button.
The lift light comes on and the lift begins its descent.
The lift arrives.
Paul gets into the lift.

Zakaria Welcome.

Paul I only have dollars. I have no change.

Paul gives him a dollar.

Sorry.

The lift door shuts.

THREE

Elena plays a sentimental pop tune arranged with trills and adornments.

Elena In the mornings after breakfast I play sentimental arrangements of European pop music to accompany the negotiations of mediocre foreign businessmen. I don't know the names of the composers. I don't know the names of the songs. Love song. Death song. Sex song. I don't even listen to them myself. I just let my fingers move across the keys and as I play I will my mind to draw out from itself the lineaments of a world in which I am playing the music of Satie for an audience of philosophers.

Zakaria prepares Arabic coffee on a metal hob on the bar.

Muna finishes her breakfast.

The television shows news images from the current situation.

Paul comes out of the lift and looks around.

First impressions.

I thought to myself, that man is an Englishman.

The suit was not pressed. The shirt was not completely clean. There was hesitation. The body language spoke of distraction and weakness.

Very English

It was not a good position from which to begin negotiations

The English are terrible negotiators. That is why they so often end up in wars.

Scottish, English, it's the same thing.

In Damascus, it is the same thing.

I don't care what you think.

I'm from the Ukraine.

Paul sits at Muna's table.

The woman?

Yes, I would say she was good looking.

Not as good looking as me.

FOUR

Paul pitches to Muna.
Paul also refers to promotional materials.
Muna holds a promotional brochure.

Paul 'Middleton Road' is a completely integrated English language learning system which takes the student from beginner to advanced level and provides a comprehensive introduction to spoken and written English as well as a working knowledge of contemporary British culture. It's a fully modular system, which means that the teacher or individual learner can learn at their own pace, but it's also linked into a wider web of knowledge resources so that the learner can pursue their own 'interest trail' throughout the whole resource package.

Beat.

You might ask – why 'Middleton Road'? Why now?

Beat.

Well, the 'Middleton Road' stories reflect a contemporary, multicultural Britain. Not the old – you know, homogenous – very much the UK now. 'Middleton Road' explores art and culture and . . .

Beat.

It's also a very friendly, natural, storytelling style. We've tried to make it as 'user-friendly' as possible, So, for example, for the younger learner, we've got Jack and Naz, the two primary schoolboys and the scrapes they get into – setting off bangers, petty shoplifting, ring-bell-run – which are more or less universal –

Beat.

And then older learners can follow the teenagers Sylvia and Duane who have a sort of . . . on-again off-again romance which takes place in a comprehensive school environment.

Beat.

The Frobishers of course, Linda and Jeff.

Jeff's always embarking on absurd projects like trying to make cider or re-enacting battles with his historical society. Linda goes to the theatre and sings in a choir . . . but they have these conversations in bed – in the evening – exploring the past tense.

'How was your day? My day was fine.'

Past imperfect. Perfect. Pluperfect.

'I *was* having a good day. I *had* sung a song with the choir when we *were* interrupted by a phone call.'

I like the Frobishers.

Beat.

Councillor Mohammed and Mrs Lyttleton provide a civics background with their endless arguments about politics and local government. So –

Beat.

You've had a chance to look at it. What do you think?

Muna What is 'ring-bell-run'?

Paul It's a . . . you ring the doorbell and then . . . Did you never do this? Maybe you don't – you ring the doorbell, then you run away and the adult opens the door and – you know – 'Grrr' – it's a form of mischief-making.

Muna OK.

Paul You probably don't have that here.
More respect.

Muna No. We have it.

Beat.

OK.
The Dean has looked at your brochure, Mr Corrigan. It is a very nice programme.

Paul Great.

Beat.

I'm not Mr Corrigan, actually. Mr Corrigan – Sean – is my boss. I'm Mr Hartstone, in fact. Sorry. My name is

Hartstone. I thought Belinda might have told you – she didn't tell you?

Muna I was told to expect Mr Corrigan of The Language Factory.

Paul He couldn't come. He's at a conference in the Caribbean. He asked me to take this meeting.

Muna Do you work for The Language Factory?

Paul Yes.

Muna In what capacity?

Paul I'm the – I wrote it. 'Middleton Road'. I wrote the stories.

Muna You wrote it?

Paul Yes.

Muna Did you do the drawings?

Paul No.

Beat.

Do you like the drawings?

Muna They're OK.

Paul I've always wished I could draw but –

You know, capture –

No.

Beat.

Muna I wondered about you. Last night. I thought, what if the airport is closed because of the situation –

Paul The situation?

Muna There was fighting in Beirut – last night. Very bad.

17

Paul Oh.

They didn't say anything about that on the plane.

Muna The situation just now is not good.

Beat.

Paul On the way here the plane stopped in Beirut. They didn't say anything about the situation.

Muna Yes.

Paul Does it stop in Beirut on the way back?

Muna Yes.

Beat.

Would you like a coffee?

Paul Thank you.

Muna What type do you want? He can do all types of coffee. Espresso. Cappuccino.

Paul What's he making now?

Muna Arabic coffee.

Paul Maybe I'll have Arabic coffee.

Muna It's very strong.

Paul Still. When in Rome.

Muna Rome?

Paul I'll have whatever you would have. What would you have?

Muna I would have camomile tea.

Paul I'm in Damascus. I have had two hours' sleep. I'm going to go mad. Go native. I'm going to have the Arabic coffee.

Muna Porter. Please. Could you bring us an Arabic coffee and a camomile tea?

Zakaria Yes, madam.

Muna English people usually ask for cappuccino.

The lift bell tings.
Wasim gets out of the lift.

Wasim Muna, darling, there you are!

Muna Here is the Dean. We can talk about the book now.

Wasim I'm starving. Where's breakfast?

Muna You're too late.

Wasim Too late?

Muna It's after ten. Breakfast's over.

Wasim For goodness sake. I told you to book The Four Seasons. At The Four Seasons you can eat until eleven-thirty.

Muna The Four Seasons costs twice the price. You're late, Wasim. I started the meeting without you.

Dean, may I present to you Paul Hartstone of The Language Factory?

Wasim Does he speak Arabic?

Muna No.

Wasim offers his hand.

Wasim Wasim Al Husseiny.

Paul Paul Hartstone.

Wasim I slept in. I was up all night writing a poem.

Muna The Dean apologises. He was working late.

Paul No problem.

Wasim An erotic poem.

Muna The Dean doesn't speak any English, but he speaks some French.

Wasim A poem about you.

Muna I don't want to hear it, Wasim.

Wasim *Parlez-vous français?*

Paul *Un peu.*

Wasim *Enchanté.*

Paul *Enchanté.*

Wasim *Vous êtes anglais.*

Paul *Oui.*

Wasim *J'adore les anglais, Monsieur, mon grand-père . . . grand-père, a tué un soldat anglais pendant le période du Mandat Britannique – à Jérusalem.*

Paul Right. It takes me a moment to get my French head on.

Muna The Dean is telling you his grandfather killed an English soldier in Jerusalem during the British Mandate.

Wasim mimes shooting at Paul.

Wasim *Et votre grand-père – a-t-il tué des Arabes?*

Muna Did your grandfather kill any Arabs?

Paul *Je pense que non.*
Non.

Wasim *Et votre fils? Peut-être maintenant en Iraq?*

Paul struggles with the French.

Muna He's speaking about Iraq.

Paul *Monsieur le Dean, les citoyens de Grande Bretagne n'aiment pas la guerre. Non. Moi je pense que la guerre dans Iraq c'est . . . un . . . un grand erreur.*

. . .

Très grand.

Sorry, my French is terrible.

Muna Yes.

Wasim sits.

Wasim Waiter – *café au lait.*

Wasim picks up a 'Middleton Road' leaflet.

Muna What do you think?

Wasim I'm finding him a little irritating.

Muna What do you think about the books?

Wasim We can't buy them.

Muna Why not?

Wasim The Ministry of Education will never let us teach them.

Muna They might. If we ask. If we make adjustments.

Wasim Forget it. Let's have our coffee and go. I've arranged to meet Khaled in the old city. His wife's a painter. You'll like her.

Muna You told me you liked this proposal.

Wasim I know.

Muna You told me to set up a meeting.

Wasim I know.

Paul What's he saying?

Muna Excuse us one moment.

Zakaria arrives with the coffee and tea.

Zakaria Scottish.

Muna Wasim.

Muna takes Wasim aside.

Zakaria Mel Gibson. *Braveheart.*

Paul Yes.

Zakaria Freedom!

Paul Yes. Freedom.

Zakaria Please sign.

Paul signs for the coffee.
   Paul gives Zakaria the receipt and a tip.

Welcome.

Zakaria returns to the bar.

Muna Have you even read the textbooks?

Beat.

Wasim!

Wasim Darling, you don't think I came all the way to Damascus to talk to an English teacher, do you?

You're annoyed.

Muna Of course I'm annoyed.

Wasim Look. I'll tell you the truth. The Minister of Education has called us in for a meeting – tomorrow. She wants to look at funding. I could have taken the Assistant Dean with me but he's hopeless. I wanted someone sharp with me. I wanted you.

Besides, tonight is the Writers' Union annual dinner.

Muna You've got it all planned out.

Wasim All the old faces will be there. Abu Amar, Khaled. I knew you'd want to go.

Muna We're supposed to be working.

Wasim Darling, it's been so long since we spent time together. Let's not waste it working.

Muna Our students don't have decent textbooks, Wasim.

Wasim There are always textbooks. There's a rep coming from Hong Kong next week. And one from Singapore. There are a hundred good language programmes we can use. It's all English, darling, It's all the same.

Muna He's come from all the way from the UK.

Wasim So he'll have a nice holiday.

Muna What am I supposed to say to him?

Wasim Anything you like, darling, I don't care.

Muna You didn't even read the books.

Wasim I trust you to do that.

Tell him whatever you want. Just make it quick. We're in Damascus – the city is ours. Let's not languish in a foyer.

Muna Mr Hartstone.

Paul Look, call me – Paul.

Muna Paul, the Dean wants you to know – this is a good moment for you to be here. The Dean wants us to update all the English-language learning systems we use in the Institute. Currently we have to use an old Russian system. It's very old-fashioned.

Paul I understand.

Muna 'Quick, Mother – the bailiff is coming – we must lock the door.'

Paul Out of date phraseology.

Muna Yes.

Paul Probably should be 'Quick, Mum, the bailiff is coming.'

Muna Exactly. The President wants our country's youth to open their arms to the English-speaking world. He wants them to be able to communicate as widely as possible.

Paul That's brilliant.

    Wasim I feel sexy.

    Muna Do you?

    Wasim Don't you?

Paul What's he saying?

Muna Nothing.

    Wasim Hotels. That's what does it. Away from home. Sitting on your bed with a bottle of whisky from the minibar waiting for the soft knock of a beautiful woman on your bedroom door. Hotels are sexy.

Muna The Dean says –

    Wasim Hotels are sexy.

Muna – contrary to what you may hear on your news media, we actually have a free education system here of a very high quality.

Paul Right.

    Wasim The endless possibilities present in every moment.

Muna That's enough.

Wasim Sorry. You're working.

Muna Students are allowed to speak their mind.

We encourage our students to question ideas – and they do. There is a big appetite for learning English. It is important for the Arab world that we have young people who are able to make their way in a globalised marketplace. That means independence of mind.

Paul Yes.

Muna Combined with a strong respect for Arabic values.

Paul I understand.

Muna So your package has arrived at an opportune moment.

Paul I'm glad.

Muna There are just a few small issues in the text and drawings which we would have to change and then we would feel able to buy your package.

Paul Right.
Mistakes?

Muna Issues.

Paul What sort of issues?

Muna Issues of cultural and political understanding.

Beat.

We have to be sensitive to the situation in the region.

Paul I see.
Tell the Dean I understand.

Wasim Do you want to see my poem?

Wasim takes out a quite nice notebook.

It's been so long I thought the impulse had gone. But last night, knowing you were in the next room, knowing we were in Damascus together again – it came back. It really did.

Muna What did?

Wasim The poetry.

Muna Excuse us a moment.

Wasim Do you want to read it?

Muna No.

Wasim I'm thinking of entering the competition tonight. Read it. Please.

Muna takes the book.
She reads.

I don't know if it's – compared to what I used to . . .
   The second line is still – and I need to work on the end . . .
   But I think – I really think I might have captured . . .

She reads on.
She closes the book.
She gives it back.

Muna It's nice.

Wasim Nice. Is that all you can say?

(*Reading.*)
'I taste the iron sharpness of blood on my tongue
As you kneel to kiss me.'

Nice.

Muna The Arabic is terrible.

Wasim It's not supposed to be pretty. It's written in the language of the street.

Muna Why did you show this to me, Wasim?

Beat.

It's not appropriate.

Wasim *Sorry.*

Paul What does the Dean say?

Muna Mr Hartstone, the Dean was reminding me that the President has said clearly that he wants our youth to open their arms to the English-speaking world.

Paul Right –

Muna But we have to be practical. Without certain adaptations to your text we can't be sure the package will be acceptable to the Education Minister. The Dean would like you and I to work through the problems. We could begin today if you like.

Beat.

Paul I'm supposed to be flying home this afternoon. My wife – I have to return to . . .

Beat.

How extensive – how far-reaching?

Muna If we make the changes now the Dean can present the programme to the Minister of Education tomorrow.

Paul I just can't stay another night away. I promised my wife –

Beat.

Sorry.

Muna That's fine.
We have to leave it.

Paul OK.

Wasim Are we done?

Muna We're done.

Wasim shakes Paul's hand and refuses to let go until the photo is taken. He gives Paul a small volume of poetry in translation.

Wasim *Monsieur Corrigan, merci beaucoup de votre présentations. C'était très intéressant. Me permettrez vous de présenter un petit volume de ma poésie – traduit en Français par moi-même –* Les Chansons Damascènes *– quelques poèmes des rues.*

Muna The Dean thanks you for your presentation which he thought was interesting. He's sorry we won't be working together. He hopes you will accept a present of his book of poems as a gesture of goodwill.

Wasim Take a photo, will you? We can put it on the office wall with the others.

Muna takes a photo.

Wasim *Au revoir Monsieur. Merci beaucoup.*

Come on, Muna darling, let's go. Damascus belongs to us.

Wasim leaves.

Paul I'm sorry.

Muna So am I.

Muna leaves.

Paul Fuck. Piss. Cock.

FIVE

Zakaria sets the tables for lunch: starched tablecloths and plastic jasmine flowers.

The television shows news images from the current situation.

Elena Lunchtime – random notes. Chopin nocturnes backwards. Boulez upside down. I read Sartre and whenever the letters a, b, c, d, e, f or g appear in the text I play that note.

Camus' *L'étranger.*

She shows you the book.

Rich women eat thin lunches and talk about building schools for the deaf and homes for the mentally enfeebled. Old men tuck in their napkins and apprise young men of that which they have observed in their long lives.

It's axiomatic in any society that people who order lunch in three-star hotels will and should be the first murdered in pursuit of revolutionary social change.

I'm a Marxist.

Aren't you?

Your should be.

You smoke like a Marxist.

Marxists and the bereaved smoke in a very similar way. They suck the smoke in deep. It's all to do with not eating. Have you been eating?

You keep thinking about him, don't you?

'What happened? What happened?' You say to yourself.

'Tell me, Elena? Tell me why?'

Elena pretends to cry.

There was a bomb.

Why?

Do you want the long answer or the short answer?

In some senses you need to go back to the carving out of
Lebanon as a Maronite Christian enclave by the French
in 1920. The French mandate locked the different
confessional communities into an unstable relationship
which –

Short answer?

Shit happens.

SIX

Lunchtime.

Paul in the foyer with his suitcase.

Zakaria You are going, Mr Paul?

Paul Not just yet, Zakaria. I've checked out. There's still
a few hours until my flight. Is it all right if I sit here for
a while?
    Until my taxi comes.

Zakaria Of course.

*Paul sits and begins to try and make himself
comfortable.*
    Zakaria returns.

You are interested in Damascus?

Paul Damascus. Yes.

Zakaria I take you to the old city. Have you been to the
old city?

Paul I haven't. No.

Zakaria I will take you to the Great Mosque.

Zakaria shows Paul a postcard from the stand.

Paul I'm sorry, Zakaria. I've had two hours' sleep. I just want to . . . chill – you know?

Zakaria Are you Christian?

Paul No.

Zakaria Jewish?

Paul No . . . I –

Zakaria Muslim?

Paul I'm agnostic.

Beat.

I have a great deal of respect for –

Zakaria Buddhist?

Paul No.

Zakaria You have no religion?

Paul I like to pray, even meditate on . . . Spirituality is . . . I think there is a spiritual dimension to –

. . .

Christian.

Zakaria You are welcome.

Paul Zakaria, I'm tired. Is it all right if I sleep here? Just for a couple of hours.

He gives Zakaria some money.

Make sure nobody steals my case.

Zakaria You are welcome.

Zakaria retreats.
Paul inflates his travel pillow.
He takes his shoes off.

Mr Paul –

Paul What?

Zakaria Do you know girls?

Paul What?

Zakaria Do you know Scottish girls?

Paul Do I know them?

Zakaria Do you bring Scottish girls with you to Damascus?

Paul What – In my suitcase?

Zakaria laughs.
Paul laughs.
Beat.

Zakaria Do you meet Scottish girls here in Damascus?

Paul Zakaria. I'm sorry. I don't meet any girls here, no.

Zakaria OK. OK.

Beat.
Paul settles in the chair, ready to sleep.

Maybe we go to the mosque. Maybe we meet girls.

Beat.

Paul Girls? In the mosque?

Zakaria Of course.

Paul You go to the mosque to pick up girls?

Zakaria Of course.

Paul Does it work?

Zakaria shrugs.

Zakaria I like to change my life. Only a little. But to change it. I like to meet girls from France. From Italy. From America. I like to find a Scottish girl to break up my life. To break it up.

Paul I know how you feel.

Zakaria Come. Mr Paul. Come to the mosque. We break up our lives.

Paul Not today, Zakaria.

Zakaria I am your guide.

Paul Sorry, Zakaria. No.

Beat.

Zakaria Scottish girls are very free, I think.

Paul Not really.

Zakaria I see Scottish girls and men play naked in the sea.

Paul You see that?

Zakaria With my own eyes.

Paul Do you mean naked or do you mean in . . . you know, thongs.

Zakaria Naked. I see it.

Paul Where?

Zakaria On the beach.

Paul It's possible.

Zakaria Scottish men and Scottish girls naked, and then when it is dark they come out of the sea. They touch each

other. They lie on the beach. The moon is big. They drink.
They smoke hashish.

Paul Do you mean Scottish girls?

Zakaria Scottish girls.

Beat.

Come to the mosque.

Paul Look Zakaria, what you've seen, it's actually quite
uncommon for Scottish girls to be naked, Zakaria.
Particularly not the ones you pick up in mosques.

Paul curls up, ready to sleep.
 *Zakaria returns with a postcard of mosaic work
from the stand.*

Zakaria In the mosque – there is mosaic. This is very old
mosaic from before Ottoman times.

Paul It's lovely.

Zakaria To make this mosaic is my father's job.

Paul Is it?

Beat.

Zakaria You are a writer, Mr Paul.

Paul Sort of. Yes.

Zakaria Are you a rich?

Paul No.

Zakaria OK.

Paul curls up, ready to sleep.
 Zakaria returns.

I am a writer, Mr Paul. I write a film script. I write a
script of my life also containing mythology. I earn how
much money for this in Hollywood?

Paul A script of your life?

Zakaria Of course.

Paul I don't know, Zakaria. Has anything happened to you in your life?

Zakaria No.

Paul Right.

Zakaria Nothing happens to me.

Paul So – reflective, then . . .

Zakaria How much money in Hollywood?

Paul I don't know the market, I'm afraid. It's not my area.

Zakaria How much?

Paul Not very much, I'm afraid.

Zakaria How much?

Paul A film script about nothing in Arabic by an unknown writer, Zakaria. That's not going to sell for a lot in Hollywood.

Zakaria How many dollars?

Paul A thousand dollars.

Zakaria One thousand dollars.

Beat.

Paul Maybe you could sell it to a Syrian company.

Zakaria OK.

Paul You should do it.

Zakaria OK.

Paul Zakaria, I need to sleep. I have a taxi coming.

Paul gives Zakaria some money.

35

Zakaria Welcome.

Zakaria goes away.
   Paul tries to get comfortable on the chair.

He curls up on the chair.

Paul's phone rings.
   He answers his phone.

Paul Sean.

Yeah, I met them . . . They want changes – changes to the text . . . I don't think we should . . . It's not lazy – it's . . . It's not lazy – I'm not being lazy . . . I don't want changes.

No, Sean, I'm coming home.

I'm coming home and, yes – yes, I may well have sex with my wife. I very much look forward to it . . . Enjoy the sunshine – you and . . . and . . . Belinda? Sean – for God's sake.

Paul ends the phone call.
   He prepares himself for sleep again.

A moment.
   Zakaria returns.

Zakaria Mr Paul. Outside. Two girls. Do you see?

Paul I see.

Zakaria These are American girls.

Paul Zakaria, I –

Zakaria Come. We will talk to them.

Paul I don't think they will want to talk to us.

Zakaria Come.

Paul No, Zakaria.

Zakaria Why not?

Paul I am a married man, Zakaria.

Zakaria It is not good to eat the same food every day.

Paul Look. You go. Zakaria. You talk to them.

Zakaria You will talk with them. We can take them to the hotel. We will play with them. Only for two days.

Paul Zakaria, if I thought your plan had even the remotest chance of success I might change my mind, but I really, really think those girls are here to have a cultural experience – and . . . You're a good looking young man – I don't think the presence of a middle-aged Scottish man is going to sway them in your favour, so – you know – go on yourself, Zakaria. Good luck to you.

Zakaria OK.

Beat.

For a visa I must have invitations. Five years since a French girl is here. Josephine. I spend a day with her. She tells me I can come and stay with her in Valence. Every year I apply for a visa. Every year the visa is not approved.

Beat.

My father makes mosaic. He is an artisan. My brother also makes mosaic.

Beat.

My brother is an engineer.

Beat.

My brother is a soldier.

Beat.

My fingers are too quick. I am not clever. I am afraid.

My brothers. They are all in the village in my father's house, all their wives, all their children. Many, many children. Everybody sits around the big table. Everybody eat and drink. I am here. In Damascus.

If I am not away from here, I am dead.

I am dead inside.

Do you know Valence?

Paul I've been there once. I drove through it.

Zakaria How is it?

Paul It seemed like a nice place.

Zakaria Do you think I can work in Valence?

Paul Maybe.

Beat.

Zakaria Those girls are very beautiful.

Paul Yes.

Zakaria What do I say to them?

Paul I don't know.

Zakaria You know.
What do I say?

Beat.

Paul OK. Look, Zakaria. Approach them and ask if they would like someone to show them around the old city. Tell them about your father making mosaics. Ask them if they are interested in more sightseeing. Show them around. Don't say anything sexual. And then, later on, if they seem relaxed, come back here with them and ask if you can buy them a drink.

Zakaria Here?

Paul Why not?

Zakaria A drink here is very expensive.

Paul OK. Look.

He gives Zakaria some more money.

Beat.

Zakaria No.

Paul Please.

Zakaria You are my friend.

Beat.

Paul withdraws the money.

Paul Of course.

Zakaria Welcome.

Zakaria goes back to the reception.

Paul curls up to sleep.
He falls asleep.

The hotel phone rings.
Zakaria answers.

OK. Yes. He is here. I will get him.

Zakaria looks at Paul.
Zakaria goes over to Paul.
He nudges him.

Paul Oh, for fuck's sake, Zakaria.

Zakaria Mr Paul. British Airways have called. There has been a bomb in the car park of Beirut Airport. Beirut Airport is closed. Your flight is cancelled.

Beat.

It is the situation.

Now you stay here one new night.

Paul Fuck. Piss. Cock.

SEVEN

Elena plays lush romantic music from films.

The television shows news images of the current situation.

Zakaria clears the tables for lunch and lays the tables for afternoon tea: cake stands with cakes; coffee and biscuits.

Elena In the afternoon I play film themes for lovers. *Titanic. Dr Zhivago. ET.*

It's quiet in the afternoons, but there are always one or two couples hanging about. Young men and their impossible girlfriends. Every young man in Damascus an impossible girlfriend – the one he loves he knows he will never be allowed to marry because she's too rich or too poor, or she's from the wrong religion or he's from the wrong family. And so they come: these desperate boys and impossible girls, and they sit and have tea and cake and – for an hour or so – they long for each other.

I play in order to make them feel sad.

It amuses me.

Muna enters.

What happened in the afternoon? It was embarrassing.

We were all talking about it.

Do I have to spell it out?

Come on.

It's obvious.

The English language is full of subtleties and confusions but the Englishman's body is as simple as a child's. In his mind his aims are complex and uncertain but his heart hides clear desires and the heart is in his body, in his eyes, in his hands, in his neck. So an Englishman's body will always point towards the thing he wants. Like a plant which always makes its shape towards the sun.

Paul shapes his body towards Muna.

I have an MA in psychology.

EIGHT

The foyer, afternoon.
Muna and Paul sit together with the 'Middleton Road' books in front of them.

Muna Chapter Eleven, page thirty-one.
The episode where Mrs Lyttleton visits Councillor Mohammed to discuss the problem of dogs barking in the night.

Paul OK. Got that.

Paul finds the page.

Councillor Mohammed talks about tolerance.

Muna That's a problem.

Paul That's a problem?

Muna Mrs Lyttleton is very aggressive. Very crazy. 'Who owns these dogs? Who is responsible? These dogs are a menace.' She wants the dogs to be locked up.

Paul But then we meet *Mrs* Mohammed and she says that the sound of the dogs makes her feel safe. Because she knows that if strangers or burglars were to come into the back yards of the terrace, then the dogs would bark.

Muna Yes, it's a very nice moral.

Paul Thank you.

41

Muna We will have a problem with this.

Paul Right.

Muna In this story Mrs Muhammad is wearing a full niqab. She is covered.

Paul Yes.

Muna The Institute is secular. We are trying to achieve equality for the women we train in all the civil services, and in education sectors especially. It would be better if Mrs Mohammed could be portrayed as a modern woman.

Paul OK.

Muna In this story the aggressive, difficult woman is uncovered and the moderate, tolerant woman is covered.

Paul But that's their characters.

Muna Why is she portrayed like this? This is very old-fashioned you know.

Paul Because it's the truth. Some women in some communities prefer to be covered.

Muna Which women? Which women prefer?

Paul It's an issue of faith.

Muna This is an issue of patriarchy.

Paul I think . . . Patriarchy?

Muna Maybe in England you want to throw away equality. Here we are trying to educate girls that they are equal. There are plenty of communities here where women are kept down by religion or tradition. If a woman teacher is in the classroom using this teaching material, her position will be undermined.

Paul I think you're overreacting.

Muna When I was growing up in Beirut my mother dressed as she pleased. She wore the latest Paris fashions. The women in Cairo, in all the big cities in Egypt, in Palestine, in Iraq could dress as they pleased. In the seventies women were finally making progress, and now in all those places they are being threatened. In Iran, in Egypt even, there can be problems for being uncovered. Iraq – which used to be very free for women – now they are being killed for even being teachers or so on.

Paul OK.
     OK.
     Maybe the episode could be a classroom talking point. Could it? A useful classroom aid.

Muna It's not good to link tolerance and fundamentalism like this. It is confusing.

Paul Mr Mohammed is not fundamentalist. He's religious. That's all.

Muna I heard on the BBC News that there was honour killing in Britain. Honour killing! We have stopped all that here. They interviewed some Muslim school pupils. They were all talking about honour honour honour. These are the words of fundamentalism. These are the codes of patriarchy. You can have this in your British textbooks but we do not want it in our textbooks.

Paul OK. I think I can maybe . . . I can talk to the illustrator.

Muna You will do this?

Paul I'll speak to him.

Muna Chapter Two, page twelve.

Paul Right.

Muna Jack discusses with his mother a problem of shoes.

Paul Trainers, yes.

Muna In this scene he is very disrespectful to his mother.

Paul Is he?

Muna He says to her, 'You're stupid. I hate you.'

Paul Yes.

Muna This is not acceptable.

Paul Yes, but Jack's being selfish in that scene. That's the point.

Muna This cannot be read out in a classroom.

Paul Really?

Muna It is too much disrespect between a child and an elder.

Paul OK. I'll look at it.

Muna Chapter Seven, page forty-four. Duane performs some music.

Paul Yes.

Muna He sings some lyrics.

Paul He writes some lyrics to a rap. It's part of the interactivity of the programme, because you can listen to the CD as part of the resource pack.

Muna The lyrics of the rap concern things he will achieve through his music. He will be famous. He will own a car, a big house. Also he will sleep with many women.

Paul He says he will have ten girlfriends.

   Beat.

He's complaining about his current situation where he has to do a paper round for money. It's his dream –

Muna This is not acceptable.

Paul Why?

Muna Individualism, materialism. These are not in line with our values.

Paul Oh, come on, credit the children with some intelligence.

Muna We can't promote individualism.

Paul It's funny. It's supposed to be – Don't you think it's funny?

Muna It's very funny.

Paul Duane is dreaming.

Muna The students who will be learning from your book. They have not got choices about which they can dream to the same extent as your character Duane. I don't want to make them feel any smaller than they already do.

Paul All right. I see.

Muna There are fourteen further instances of individualistic behaviour which I have identified.

Paul OK. I'll look at them.

Muna Chapter Nine, Sylvia and Duane Kiss.

Paul OK. I understand.

Muna Teachers here can be very conservative.

Paul It's fine.

Muna It's OK to know that they are in love.

Paul Honestly, I understand.

Muna It's a very sweet story.

Paul It's innocent.

Muna But you must understand that here a boy and girl would not have any kind of a physical relationship until they were married.

Paul Right. Really nothing?

Muna Of course.

Paul Nothing at all?

Muna Nothing.

Paul Surely behind the bike sheds . . .

Muna Bike sheds?

Paul I mean young people must find places to be with each other.

Muna No.

Paul Did you . . . I mean – when you were young did you –

Muna Did I what?

Paul Where did you – you know . . .

Muna No.

Paul Make love.

Muna In Moscow.

Paul Moscow?

Muna I had a lover in Moscow. We were students at the same university. We lived together in a shared room in an apartment. But when we came home, we had to separate. He was from a different sect.

Paul It's quite romantic.

Muna It's quite ridiculous.

Paul Moscow in the eighties.

Muna It was a nice time for me. I felt very free.

Beat.

Paul Your lover – is he . . . ?

Muna He married someone else.

Beat.

Chapter Thirty-Three, page one hundred and twenty.
This chapter is a problem.

Paul The chapter about local elections.

Muna There are a number of issues.

Mr and Mrs Frobisher sit in bed and discuss the parties they voted for that day.

Paul They also describe the different parties they *would* have voted for *had* the situation been different.

Muna ' "If they had had a different policy on recycling, I would have voted for the Conservatives," said Mr Frobisher.'

'The Liberals were going to change their policy when budget cuts meant they had to think again.'

Paul I like the Frobishers.

Muna We have to adapt this section.

Paul Adapt?

Muna We have to give different names to the political parties.

Paul Why?

Muna There are six legal parties. These are the only parties to which we can refer in educational materials.

Beat.

Paul I can't put in the names of parties which don't exist in Britain.

Muna Why not?

Paul Any student would see through it.

Muna Simply change it to Socialist Party and Nationalist Party.

Paul It would be absurd.

Muna You must have a Socialist Party in England?

Paul Not exactly.

Muna I want the students to learn English. I want them to be exposed to the internet and to debate with people from all over the world. I want them to have the best resources from which to learn, but we are working within a framework which is that our government is in a state of emergency.

Paul Your government is censoring free expression.

Muna My government is at war.

Paul Your government is a dictatorship.

Muna That is too strong.

Paul Is it?

Muna Our country is surrounded by war in Iraq, Palestine, Lebanon . . . Israel occupies our land. America calls us evil. We have many minorities here and we all live in peace and stability. There is very little crime. There are schools and universities and all the time there are fundamentalists trying to – you have to understand the context in which we are living.

Paul I'm sorry. I really don't feel comfortable with this process.

Muna I'm sorry you don't feel comfortable.

Paul I can accommodate some of the changes you're asking for, but democracy is central to –

Muna Blessed democracy. Holy democracy.

Beat.

Paul What's wrong with democracy?

Muna Your democracy is my problem.

Paul How do you make that out?

Muna Your democracy invaded Iraq.

Paul Iraq is not a popular war. That's a different thing.

Muna You had a democratic election. Why did your democratic electorate not remove the government that executed this unpopular war?

Paul The election wasn't really about the war. It was about the economy.

Beat.

Besides, the Tories were just awful at that point. Really really hopeless.

Muna You voted for Blair?

Paul I voted Labour.

Muna You had no choice?

Beat.

This year in Damascus, your embassy hosted a conference on human rights. I attended this. Professors from the UK came here to Damascus to talk to us about human rights! Ridiculous.

Paul Yes.
Is it?

Muna After Balfour – after Sykes-Picot – after Mossadeq – after Suez – and always always support for Israel – after Guantanamo – after Iraq . . . After all this *you* are coming here to lecture *us* about human rights.

Paul Right.

Muna After your allies, the Americans, send their prisoners to us in unmarked planes for torture.

Paul Point taken.

Muna You come to tell us how to live.

Paul Look, I agree. It's terrible. I'm terrible. Britain's terrible.

Muna You British. You English.

Paul I didn't vote for – I don't – I . . .

Muna Everything is your fault.

Beat.

I'm joking.

It is important that we learn about human rights.

She smiles.
He smiles.

Paul OK, look, maybe there's a way we can change the political parties. Can we give the candidates' names? 'I would have voted for Mr Smith but . . . I had voted for Mrs Brown when . . .' Would that be acceptable?

Muna This would be acceptable.

Paul OK.

Muna Last issue. Chapter Thirty-Five, page seven.

Paul Duane buys some rock and roll records from Rabbi Samuels.

Muna Yes.

Paul What?

Muna Rabbi Samuels says that he is selling his things because he is emigrating to live with his mother.

Paul Yes.

Muna The implication is that he is emigrating to Israel.

Paul No.

Muna I think it is clear.

Paul No. It think it is not clear, and even if it was –

Muna In educational materials we cannot discuss Israel without giving it a proper context.

Paul Rabbi Samuels doesn't 'discuss Israel', he just says he is going to a sunnier place.

Muna The Israeli flag is on a badge on his jacket.

Paul Is it?

Muna It's small, but you can see it.

Paul looks.

Paul Look, I didn't do the drawings.

Muna Where is he emigrating to, then? Where does he go with his mother? Where did you intend?

Paul What context do we need for Rabbi Samuels to discuss Israel?

Muna The context of explaining the illegal Zionist colonisation and campaign of occupation against the people of Palestine.

Beat.

Paul Are you serious?

Muna We just have to be practical. I just want you to edit the text a little.

Paul I understand the practicalities, but just for a moment . . . Just for a moment – let's imagine there were no practicalities. Imagine there was just you and me and – and the youth who want to open their arms to the English-speaking world. Would you edit the text then?

Beat.

I know Rabbi Samuels. He is a nice man. He used to live few doors down from me. He ran a rock and roll disco for the over-fifties in the community centre. He told me he once played bass for Herman's Hermits, I don't know if I believed him. He made friends with the black kids. He gave them records.

Rabbi Samuels did emigrate to Israel.

That's the truth.

Muna Rabbi Samuels is just a means by which you explore the future tense.

Beat.

'I look forward to walking along the beach in the sunshine with my mother.' 'I will remember you.' 'I will not need these records.'

Beat.

What is so special about your book that it cannot be touched?

Beat.

The beach along which Rabbi Samuels *will* walk with his mother *will* be a beach along which my mother *will* never walk because even though she was born in Jaffa in 1942 she was expelled by the Israelis in 1948 and she *will* never be allowed back in. And I am never *going* to see the house in which she was born. Maybe Rabbi Samuels *will* live in it.

That's the truth.

Beat.

Paul OK. OK.

No, you're right.

It must be – annoying. Having a . . . me – come here and –

Blabbering on about truth –

You're right.

It's just language.

I'll speak to Mr Corrigan. We'll mark up these changes for the Damascus edition. I can get the material to you for next – let's see – March.

I'll speak to the illustrator about the flag.

Beat.

Muna Don't.

Paul Don't what?

Muna Don't speak to the illustrator. Not yet.

Paul You don't want to change it?

Muna No.

Paul But you just said . . . the Dean said –

Muna When the Dean first came to he taught us Verlaine and Rimbaud and Genet and Fanon. He said we ought to live as if we were citizens of a country of the imagination. That we ought to live according to that country's laws. 'Let the censor come and find us, Muna. We will not do his job for him. And, who knows, when he comes calling, maybe we will be far away.'

Paul Far away.

Muna Tonight the Dean is reading his poetry at a restaurant in the old city. With his colleagues from the Writers' Union. We could go.

Paul Right. A poetry reading.

Muna If we can persuade the Dean ,maybe he will take the textbook to the Minister tomorrow as it is – unchanged.

Paul Persuade him?

Muna We could make a stand.

Paul For – freedom of –

Muna Exactly!

Paul Right.

Muna Would you like to make a stand?

Paul That would be –

Yes.

I would like that very much.

NINE

The television shows news images of the current situation.

Zakaria clears the tables and prepares for the evening.

A glitterball spins over the small dance floor

A neon sign saying JET SET LOUNGE *is lit up over the piano.*

Elena plays disco arrangements of nineteenth-century romantic composers.

Elena At night – Mozart, Weber, Schumann, Sibelius, Rimsky-Korsakov arranged in the style of light euro-pop.

They come to dance. Young married couples mostly. He works for the security services or the police, she's maybe a teacher or an engineer. They have a bit of money. They take weekends in Beirut. They spend summer in his father's village up in the mountains. They both know how lucky they are. They both know how fragile their luck is. She keeps her jewellery in a small box under the floor and he's worked out how best to pack the car in a hurry – where there's a radio, where there's a torch and a gun. At weekends they dance close on the dance floors of small city hotels and they hold each other tight. You know the type. He keeps an eye on the satellite channels and she keeps an eye on the door.

Shhhh.

The hotel is bugged.

Don't worry, nobody actually listens to the tapes.

Unless something happens.

Shhhh.

Paul enters in a hurry.

Zakaria Mr Paul. Mr Paul.

Paul Zakaria.

Zakaria I wait for you.

Paul Right, I just need to –

Zakaria The American girls come here soon.

Paul Right. The American girls. Can this wait, Zakaria, I'm bursting for a piss –

Zakaria One moment please, Mr Paul. The girls. I speak with them in the mosque. I show them the mosaic. I take them around the souk. I say to them I buy you a drink. They say they will come here tonight.

Paul That's great, Zakaria, where's the toilet?

Zakaria Toilet this way.

Paul Thank you.

Paul starts to go. Zakaria stops him.

Zakaria One moment.

Paul What?

Zakaria American girls need room, Mr Paul.

Paul Room?

Zakaria Two girls. Two rooms. You with one girl, me with other girl.

Paul What? Christ. Let's – Zakaria – I don't know if I can. Let's see what happens when they get here, yeah? It'll be fine.

Zakaria You do this. You take two rooms.

Paul What?

Zakaria You take two rooms. Or else no girls.

Paul Right.

Zakaria They are American.

Paul OK. Zakaria. OK. I'll – I'll work it out. It'll be fine.

Zakaria Fine?

Paul I'll sort it out for you. Don't worry.

Paul touches Zakaria's shoulder.

Zakaria I don't worry.
  You are my friend.

Paul Now where's the toilets?

Zakaria points off to the toilets.

Thank you.

Paul goes off.

Zakaria dances for a moment, on his own.

European dancing becomes Arab dancing.

Just for a second it's possible to believe that Zakaria will get laid tonight.

TEN

Wasim and Muna enter from the street and sit by the dance floor.

Wasim Beer.

Zakaria stops dancing and goes to pour a beer.

Thank God that's over.

Beat.

Did you see Abu Amar? He looks terrible. His face is grey and puffy and he was wheezing like a dying horse. He told me his heart valves were fucked. All night he was breathing in my left ear, 'Do you think they will invite me to Dubai, to the poetry festival in Dubai, the one you went to, will you put a word in for me, Wasim, will you, you must know the judges? Might they invite me to Dubai?'

Beat.

He used to be a beautiful man. He used to have grace.

Beat.

Even if I knew the judges, which I don't, and even if I did put a word in, which I can't, and then assuming they gave a damn about my opinion, which they wouldn't – the airline would never let him on the bloody plane.

Beat.

All the old men. All around me, old men in brown suits.

Beat.

In 1982 in the old French café on Maysaloun Street we used to stay up late and argue about whether a revolutionary art demanded new forms.

Tonight they spent the whole evening criticising the food.

Beat.

Olive trees and oceans lapping Jaffa's forlorn shore and martyrs killed for justice and the moon shining silver on the endless road to Jerusalem.

Beat.

Complacent – lazy –

Beat.

Martyrs killed for beautiful justice? Are they? Or are they just killed? Are they just killed by bullets? And as they die what thoughts go through their heads? Thoughts of beautiful justice? Or shock at the taste of their own blood.

Beat.

The ocean lapping Jaffa's forlorn shore.

Beat.

Between them those old men have conjured a wonderful country full of olive trees and grandmothers and now they live in it – in permanent exile.

Beat.

Where are the poems of the street?
  Of these streets?
  Of now?

Beat.

We are spent volcanoes.
  All of us.

  Wasim drinks his beer.
  Muna looks at him.

Muna You sound like you wanted to win the prize.

Wasim That ludicrous piece of tin. A medal with a ribbon. Khaled looked like a clown standing up there to receive it. Pretending he didn't like getting his picture taken. Did you notice the way he touched up his hair? The vanity. I don't know what was making him so happy. I would have thought that winning a state prize like that would be the very definition of failure.

Muna I liked Khaled's poem.

Wasim Of course you did, darling. You are always seduced by language.

  Paul comes back from the toilet.

Paul Muna.
  Dean.
  Amazing.
  Truly.
  Something wonderful has just happened.

Zakaria, pour me a malt whisky.

Zakaria pours a whisky for Paul.

Muna What is it?

Paul My sense of smell. I thought I'd lost my sense of smell. But just then, in the urinals, it came back.

Muna In the urinals?

Paul Excuse me.
Sign it to the room.

Paul smells the whisky.

Glorious.
Iodine and wood,
Seaweed, salt,
Islay.

Paul drinks.

Lagavulin. Caol Ila.
Where is it from?

Zakaria India.

Paul India. Amazing. Here have one yourself. And one for the Dean and one for Muna.

Zakaria pours.

What a wonderful evening. Thank you, Muna. *Merci, Monsieur Dean.* To be amongst such inspiring people. Poets and novelists and actors and the chance to see the wonderful old city.

Wasim What's he going on about?

Muna He's saying he had a nice time.

Wasim I'll bet he did. The attention you were giving him.

Muna I was helping translate, that's all.

Paul I propose a toast.

Muna He wants to propose a toast.

Wasim I propose the Englishman finally fucks off and leaves us alone.

Paul A toast to Damascus.

Muna *and* **Paul** To Damascus.

Wasim Damascus.

Paul Oh, bollocks.

Muna What?

Paul sniffs the whisky.

Paul It's gone again.

He sniffs again.

Nothing.

Muna Never mind.

Paul I come all the way to Damascus, walk through the spice souk, stand under a jasmine tree, eat oranges and roast meat, and the only odour I will remember is the smell of a communal toilet.

Muna Poor you.

Paul Maybe if I go back to the toilet I can activate it again.

Paul goes to the toilet.

Wasim and Muna listen to the music.

Beat.

Wasim Dance, come.

Muna No.

Wasim You were always the best dancer.

Muna Wasim.

Wasim Muna, do you have any idea how beautiful you are?

Muna Don't be ridiculous.

Wasim I'm not being ridiculous, I'm being very serious.

Muna Please, Wasim, don't. It's bad enough you tricked me into coming here.

Wasim It isn't just your physical beauty, Muna, that draws men towards you – although your face, your lips, your breasts, and the way your hair falls, all of those things seem almost eternally perfect – but no, it isn't those things which draw men towards you.

Muna No –?

Wasim It's the way your eyes betray you when you speak.

Muna Oh, really?

Wasim You make a castle of your speech and you hide yourself amongst its towers and battlements – but your eyes are traitors. Sending out signals to the besieging forces. I'm here. Come in. Rescue me.

Beat.

We were good together.

We were good.

Muna, darling, sleep with me tonight.

Paul returns.

Paul It's back.

He sniffs the whisky.

Thank God for that.
I went in and sniffed and it reactivated again.
What a relief.

Muna Yes. It must be.

Beat.

Paul I want to talk to the Dean about the textbooks.

Muna The textbooks?

Paul Making a stand.

Muna OK.

Paul I want to speak to him now. I've been thinking.
Will you translate? (*To Wasim.*) Dean – we'd like to talk
to you about 'Middleton Road'.

Muna Paul wants to talk to you about the programme.

Wasim 'Paul'? – He wants to fuck you.

Paul Will you translate? I don't think my French is up to it.

Muna Of course.

Wasim Do you want to fuck him?

Muna looks away.

Muna Begin.

Paul Mr Dean, tonight, as we walked through the streets
of the old city. Through the souk, through the alleys and
small squares. I noticed the way that this city has been
formed by layers and layers of accretions growing slowly
over time. But the centre of it all, the foundations upon
which everything else has grown, is the mosque. The
mosque which they tell me was once a church and once
even a Roman temple.

Do you want to translate?

Muna Paul, where is this going?

Paul Give me a chance.

> **Muna** He says that he noticed the old city. The way it's built by things being added on to each other. All higgledy-piggledy. All built around the mosque.

> **Wasim** What's his point?

> **Muna** I'm not sure.

Paul And it occurred to me that this old city, with all its interconnections and its accretions, was, in fact, a very human space. A very comfortable space in which to live. A place of infinite possibility.

> **Muna** He liked it being higgledy-piggledy. He thought it would be a nice place for humans to live.

> **Wasim** Depends how much money you have. Whether you like indoor plumbing. One of the new apartments in the suburbs outside the city might be cheaper.

Paul And then tonight, amongst all the writers, listening to them speak about their writing, it occurred to me that literature follows the same pattern, built of accretions and extensions, bits piled on top of each other, some parts crumbling away and others restored.

> **Muna** He says that for him literature is like buildings piled on top of each other.

Paul Writing is like an old city, and in its centre there is not a mosque or a temple, but something like a mosque or a temple –

> . . .

The truth.

> . . .

The desire to tell the truth.

Muna That's really hard to translate.

Paul Do you want me to rephrase it?

Muna Yes please.

Paul Writing is like Damascus.

Muna OK.

He says, writing is like Damascus.

Wasim How much more of this do I have to endure?

Paul Mr Dean, surely, your students have the right to live in Damascus. A Damascus of the mind.

Wasim What does this have to do with teaching English as a foreign language?

Paul Did he get that?

Muna What?

Paul The bit about living in Damascus.

Muna Yes. That's clear.

Wasim What's he saying?

Muna He's saying our students have a right to access writing built on the truth. He suggests that if you start off with that principle, then writing and teaching can layer itself around the truth to make something like a city – a world which the student's mind can inhabit and explore. Wandering far and wide but always coming back to truth. But if you build your writing around politics – if you start of with expediency– then . . . then the city will be full of illusion and the student will get lost

Wasim Why is he telling me this?

Muna You know why.

Wasim Do I?

Muna Of course you do.

Beat.

Wasim Muna, translate this for me please.

Muna The Dean asks me to say –

Wasim You know nothing about the country I live in. You know nothing about how it has been formed. You know nothing of its complexities and conflicts. You come here with all the shine of your English education, so certain of your values, and you lecture me about truth. Translate.

Muna You don't understand the situation. It's complicated. You come here and speak to him with certainty. He doesn't like that.

Wasim Fuck you.

Muna Just emphasis.

Wasim There is no such thing as freedom of speech. What you are defending is simply your English power to describe the status quo in whatever way you like.

Muna There are two sides to every story.

Wasim Nothing has brought more blood to this region than Anglo-Saxon idealism. You make your accommodations with your regime and I will make my accommodations with mine.

Muna He's not keen to accept the programme.

Paul Oh.

Wasim Did you tell him this?

Muna Yes.

Wasim OK?

Paul OK.

Wasim *Me comprenez vous?*

Paul *Oui. Je comprends.*

Wasim *Bien.*

Paul Sorry.

Muna It's not your fault.

> *Paul drinks his whisky.*
> *Sniffs.*
> *Notices his sense of smell has gone again.*

Paul It's gone. I'll just –

Muna Sure.

> *Paul leaves for the toilet.*

Muna You're such a hypocrite, Wasim. I could bear it if I thought that you actually believed in the struggle, the regime, the glorious motherland, but you don't. You know it's fiction, you know – we all know we know, but we just pretend.

You used to care.

Wasim I still do.

Muna Do you?

Wasim I went to prison.

Muna Six months in prison and you've been living off it for fifteen years.

Wasim If it were a bigger cause – a novel, a poem . . .

> *Paul returns.*
> *He sniffs his whisky.*
> *He drinks.*
> *Relieved.*

Paul What's he saying?

Muna Nothing. He's saying nothing.

Muna Excuse me.

Wasim What?

Muna I'm going outside to smoke.

Wasim Why don't you smoke here?

Muna I want to breathe some fresh air.

Muna gets up and leaves.

Wasim *Elle est très belle. Non?*

Paul *Belle?*

Wasim Muna.

Paul *Ah . . . oui. Oui. Très . . . belle.*

Wasim *Vous êtes marié?*

Paul *Moi. Oui.*

Beat.

Wasim *Quand on est jeune la vie semble pleine de possibilité, n'est ce pas ? Mais maintenant – la vie s'evanouit. La mort s'approche de nous à grand vitesse.*

Paul I'm sorry I don't – *oui.*

Wasim *Quel âge as-tu?*

Paul *Moi. J'ai trente-huit ans.*

Wasim *Après trente-cinq ans –*

Paul After thirty five –

Wasim *Votre chemin est décidé.*

Paul Your railway – railway? – road is decided.

Wasim *Tous les jours ce'est la même chose.*

Paul The same – the days are the same.

Wasim *Quand la mort te reclames.*

Paul When love reclaims me? *L'amor?*

Wasim *La mort.*

Paul When death reclaims me.

Wasim *Qui tu n'as pas penser –*

Paul I will arrive at death –

Wasim *Ni à ton œuvre –*

Paul Not of my work.

Wasim *Ni à ta femme.*

Paul Not of my wife.

Wasim *Ni à tes enfants –*

Paul Not of my children.

Wasim *Mais tu vas penser à la femme –*

Paul But I will think of the women? The woman –

Wasim *Qui tu n'as pas baisée.*

Paul I did not kiss? Did not fuck.

    Beat.

Eh. Oui.
   C'est vrai.

   Wasim leaves to the toilet.
    Zakaria approaches Paul.

Zakaria Mr Paul.

Paul Zakaria.

Zakaria I call the American girls.

Paul You call them?

Zakaria Yes. There is no answer.

Paul Maybe they've switched their phone off.

Zakaria Please call the American girls.

Paul I don't really want to do that.

Zakaria Please, Mr Paul.

Paul OK.
OK.

Zakaria Here.

Zakaria hands him his phone.

Paul It's ringing.
. . .
It's the answerphone.
. . .
Hello, you don't know me, I'm a friend of Zakaria?
I think you may have met him in the mosque this
afternoon. He's wondering if you want to come up to the
hotel for a drink.

Zakaria Ask them if they want to sleep with me.

Paul Zakaria doesn't know I'm saying this, but I think it
would mean a lot to him if you came up here. Even just
to help him practise his English.
OK.
Thanks.
Bye.

Zakaria Do you ask them to sleep with me?

Paul I asked them to come down for a drink.

Zakaria Welcome.

Muna returns.

Muna It's cold out there. I need to warm up.

Paul Would you like another whisky?

Muna Of course. When in Rome.

Paul What? Oh.

Muna You are Scottish. A Scottish Roman.

Paul Yes –
Zakaria. Two whiskies please.

Zakaria Yes, Mr Paul.

Beat.

Paul Muna –
I'm a little drunk, but . . . not drunk, intoxicated – on
the whisky and the old city and –

Muna It's snowing outside.

Paul It's snowing?
What do you mean?

Muna Snow.

Paul The same as –

Muna The same.

There's snow on the mountain.

Beat.

Come.

She gets up. Paul follows. Muna shows him.

Paul I can't believe there's actually snow.

Muna It happens.

Paul You think of here, you think of the desert. I think
of the desert.

Muna Sometimes it happens.

Paul It's beautiful.

Muna takes Paul's hand.
She moves towards him.
She kisses him.
Muna pulls away from the kiss.

Paul moves to kiss her.

They kiss.
He inhales, smells her hair.

Wasim returns.

Paul I want to smell your perfume.

Muna I'm not wearing perfume.

Paul No, you – I want to smell you – your hair, your skin –

Muna Where are you going?

Paul goes to the toilets.

Paul I'm going to take a big sniff of piss.

Wasim exits.

Paul exits.

ELEVEN

The glitterball starts to move and the disco lights get going.
Elena plays Arabic pop music.

Elena At precisely midnight, every night, for one hour
I play high-octane versions of Arabic pop classics.

I find the noise unbearable but they do love to dance, the
Damascenes.

It takes them out of themselves.

Muna dances.

Even Damascenes need to lose themselves from time to time.

Paul returns.
He watches Muna dancing.

Muna Come, dance.

Paul No.
No.
I'm embarrassed.

Muna Dance.

Paul I'll watch you.

Muna dances.

Elena I play all the big hits and then when everybody is dancing and the floor is full I unleash the songs of the motherland.

And they dance, with their arms in the air lost in themselves, far away.

TWELVE

Paul makes a call on his mobile.

Paul Hi, it's me.
Are you there?

Happy Valentine's Day.

If you're in bed don't pick up, don't worry. It's snowing in Damascus so . . . The plane is cancelled again – mad . . . It looks like I'll have to stay another day – just one more day.

Elena So a man lies to his wife.

People lie.

Paul Well, I hope everything's all right.
Night-night.

Paul ends the phone call.

Elena Could someone ever comprehend all the angles of your life? All your lies and stories? And, even if they could, how would they know which of your lies you believed and which you told to please your lover or which you simply entertained for an afternoon in a fit of whimsy. Notice how we always let the worst act define the life, the infidelity defines the marriage, the pornographic film defines the actress – but what about the thousand nights of fidelity, what about the films she made later in her career?

Paul Fuck piss cock.

Elena Don't make that face.

That – (*She makes a face.*)

If it hadn't have snowed nothing would have happened.

What can I say?

This is Damascus.

Sometimes it snows.

Sometimes things happen.

Sometimes people die.

End of Act One.

Act Two

ONE

The foyer, morning.

The television shows news images of the current situation.

Muna eats a breakfast of pitta bread, yoghurt, tomato, cucumber and coffee.

Elena plays and sings 'Amazing Grace'.

Elena After breakfast – ten minutes of rousing hymns to drive the last of the diners out of the room.

Come on. Out, out – Go on – get out. Go on. Away.

There's nothing to see here.

Muna moves to the comfortable seats.

Zakaria clears her table.

Nothing to see.

Morning.

Do you want a fag?

Elena offers a cigarette.

I used to love the first cigarette of the day before I became a Christian.

I'm a Christian Marxist.

Orthodox.

Both.

Transsexual.

Damascus is a place of changes.

75

You stayed last night, didn't you?

One more night.

You stood at the window and looked out at the view over Mount Quissoon. You sat on the bed. You tried to imagine he was in the room with you but you just couldn't see his face, couldn't conjure his body, and when you realised that he was no longer tangible to you – you ached but were too exhausted to cry, and so you said to yourself, 'I'm just wrung out. Wrung out like a dish rag.' Didn't you?

And you prayed, didn't you?

Even though you no longer believe in God, you prayed.

These are the sorts of things I know.

Zakaria goes behind the reception desk and lies down.

TWO

Paul enters from the street.
He is carrying a red Dansette record player.

Paul Zakaria?
Zakaria?

Paul looks for Zakaria.

Caught you.

Zakaria appears from behind the desk where he has been sleeping.

Zakaria Mr Paul?

Paul One Arabic coffee, please.

Zakaria prepares an Arabic coffee.

Were you asleep?

Zakaria Yes.

Paul Late night?

Zakaria Yes.

Paul You have a very busy lifestyle, Zakaria.

Zakaria Yes.

Paul Quite the man about town.

Zakaria Yes.

Paul Gadding about from girl to girl.

Zakaria Yes.

Paul Are you all right, Zakaria?

Zakaria Yes.

Paul You seem – angry.

Zakaria I am angry, Mr Paul. Last night I wait for the American girls. I wait here for them. At two a.m. the American girls come.

Paul They turned up?

Zakaria They come here, it is two a.m.

Paul I ooo.

Zakaria First they are at the English pub, they are drunk.

Paul Right. That's good, isn't it?

Zakaria They are drunk and they laugh. They talk very fast and they laugh. Now they ask for you. Now they want to see you. Now they say you have a sexy Scottish voice.

Paul Right.

Zakaria I tell them you sleep. They drink more. They are very free girls. I give drinks to them gratis. They say,

77

'Zakaria, do you want to practise your English?' I say of course. They tell me to say curse words.

They tell me to say 'fuck', 'cock','pussy', 'ass', 'dick', 'cunt', 'titty'.

I say those words and they laugh. I am tired, Mr Paul. I am working. I don't want to say curse words. I ask the American girls, 'Would you like to sleep with me?' Then they laugh. They say you phone them. They say you tell them I want to practise English.

Paul Right.

Zakaria I do not want to practise English, Mr Paul.

Paul No.

Zakaria I want to sleep with girls.

Paul Right.

Zakaria What I say I want – that is what I want. Not what you say I want.

Paul Yes. I'm sorry.

Zakaria I want to break up my life.

Zakaria gives Paul his coffee.

Paul I'm sorry.
Look, Zakaria, I'm really sorry.

Zakaria Sign for coffee please.

In the night I go to my friend Kemal. I find him. I wake him up. He say to me: 'Zakaria stop seeing foreign women. Stop helping foreign men. Zakaria, start to help yourself.'

Paul That's good advice.

Muna and Paul see each other.

Muna Paul.

Paul Good morning.

Muna Morning.

Paul Watching television.

Muna It's terrible.

Paul Yes.

Muna The child. The child on the news. Did you see?

Paul Yes.

Muna It's so sad.

Paul Her face. The way she holds on to her father. It's – it's just . . .

Silence.

Muna You've been shopping.

Paul Souvenir.

Muna touches the record player.

Muna I haven't seen one of these since I was nine years old.

Paul I found it in an antique shop in the old city – they're very expensive now. To see one – I had to buy it.

Muna My brother used to have one just like it. If I wanted to play a song I had to go to his room and knock on his door. He was older than me. He bought the records. I remember standing in the doorway. 'Selim . . . Selim . . . let me play Fairouz. Let me play the record.' Sometimes he would let me.

Paul Muna, last night – what happened between us . . .

Muna Was it expensive?

Paul What?

Muna The record player.

Paul I don't know.

Muna How much?

Paul A thousand.

Muna Did you negotiate a price?

Paul Not really.

Muna You should have negotiated.

Paul I don't like to.

Muna You should.

Paul Should I?

Muna The trader expects it.

Paul Does he?

Muna If you don't negotiate, he thinks he's set the price too low.

Paul Does he?

Muna If you don't negotiate, he thinks you are showing off.

Paul I got him down from one thousand two hundred.

Muna If he started at one thousand two hundred then you could have taken him down to five hundred.

Paul I don't care about the price of the record player.

Beat.

Muna.

Muna Don't –

Paul Last night – I want to say –

Muna Please don't say.

Beat.

Let me see the records. Which records did you buy?

Paul I didn't buy them – he just gave me a box.

He brings out the box.
She looks through them.

Muna Ahh. Marcel, Abdel Khelim, Fairouz! You got Fairouz. I love Fairouz . . . Let me see which ones –

Paul You know all these?

Muna Of course.

She picks out a single.

I used to listen to this in Beirut. We would drive down to the beach and Selim would bring the record player and sit it between me and him on the back seat of my father's car, and then when we got to the beach he would lay out a cloth and put it down. My brother was very handsome. I felt so proud to dance with him. I thought every girl on the beach would be so jealous of me dancing with handsome Selim.

You like to listen.

Paul Do I?

Muna Letting me talk.

Paul I'm interested.

Muna Maybe you're a spy.

Paul I'm not a spy.

Muna Are you sure?

Paul I'm a TEFL teacher.

Muna That would be a good disguise for a spy.

Beat.

Paul I didn't know you were from Beirut.

Muna I lived in Beirut. Until I was thirteen years old.

Paul How did you end up here?

Muna My mother and father were Jaffa. After Israel invaded the West Bank in 1967 they moved to Beirut. They wanted to carry on the struggle. They were very political. Very strict. Strict nationalists. Strict Communists. Strict feminists.

Paul They sound like fun.

Muna They were fun.

In 1975 the civil war started in Lebanon, all the different forces on all the different sides. Christian. Shia. Sunni. The Palestinians were in the middle of it all. Eventually the Israelis invaded and occupied Lebanon. They invaded Beirut to drive out the PLO.

My mother and father and I – we had to find somewhere else to live.

Paul What happened to your brother?

Muna My brother was a fighter.

Paul Right.

   Beat.

He was the same age as my students. I see a boy in the cafeteria sometimes. The girls love him. He's good looking. They hang on his words. I see Selim. I look at the boys and they seem so young and soft and silly. To think of them with guns, fighting from house to house against tanks and – everything.

Listen to me.

I'm like Mrs Frobisher in your book.

Paul Are you?

Muna Always exploring the past tense.

   Beat.

Paul Muna – last night . . .

Muna You're very stubborn.

Paul Something happened between us.

Muna You're determined to say things out loud.

Paul Last night we made a connection.

Muna Like electricity.

Paul Something happened between us and –

Muna Just saying it out loud doesn't make it true.

Paul It doesn't make it true but it is a good test.

Like knocking on a wall to feel if it's hollow.

Something happened between us.

Something happened.

Muna?

Didn't it?

Muna Can I put on the record?

Paul Of course.

She puts on the record.
The record plays
They listen.

Muna Dance.

Paul I'm embarrassed.

Muna Don't be.

She takes his hand.
Pulls him to his feet.

Make eye-contact.

Paul I feel –

Muna Eyes. Eyes.

Paul I –

Muna Don't speak.

Eyes.

Paul Eyes.

They dance.

Muna That's it.

A moment.
Muna goes very close.

Paul thinks it's a kiss.

She withdraws.

Muna takes the record off.

Paul Last night something happened.

Muna Past perfect.

Paul Something is happening.
Present imperfect.

Muna Sometimes things happen.
Present perfect.
Complete.

Paul Last night I couldn't sleep. I kept thinking of you.
Wondering if I should find your room. Wondering if you'd
find mine. After some time I heard the dawn prayer.
I looked out of the window and I watched the sun rise.
The light made the snow pink on the rooftops. I went out
into the streets for a walk and the streets were covered in
a thin layer of frozen snow. I walked into the old city and
I just wandered about. I let myself get lost. Sometimes I was
making the first footsteps. Down every alley and turn
I would find another alley and turn. I thought I'd never
find my way out again, but whichever way I went I always
ended up at back at the mosque, and in the end I thought
I would go inside.

Just thinking 'to look' – just thinking 'to experience'.

So I went to the gate and the man said take off your shoes – because of course you have to take off your shoes – and so I took off my shoes and I walked barefoot across the snow-covered courtyard, felt my feet in the snow. I looked up at the sky and I saw it full of starlings wheeling and I noticed that the mosque walls framed the bright blue empty sky as if to say – this blue is the image of God. I went into the main hall of the mosque and I was surprised because it was so big and so empty. Just a high-ceilinged pillared room about the size of a football pitch.

Empty space.

The floor was covered in hundreds of Persian rugs.

My feet felt warm on the rugs.

A few men prayed. A few women sat on low benches. Some children ran about playing. Their voices echoing about the hall.

I thought, I'll just see – just see what happens –
    If I stay here for a while.
    So I did.
    And something did happen – I realised –

Something of a pause.

In the end, Muna there's only the present moment.
    Now.
    I want you.

Muna You left.

Paul Right.

Muna I have to go. The Dean and I have a meeting with the Deputy Minister for Education. You are leaving this afternoon.

Paul Tomorrow morning.

Muna But your flight is this afternoon.

Paul Last night I called my wife. I told her that the plane was cancelled.

Muna I'll be back here at seven.

Paul I'll be here.

We'll go to the old city.

We'll have dinner.

I'll stay the night.

Muna Now you're exploring the future tense.

Muna kisses him on the cheek.
She leaves to go to the street.

Paul puts another record on the Dansette.
Zakaria approaches Paul.
He has a polythene bag full of papers.

Zakaria Mr Paul.

Paul Yes?

Zakaria I bring you my life.

He shows Paul the bag.

Paul What?

Zakaria The script of my life also containing mythological elements.

Paul You wrote a script?

Zakaria Of course.

Paul I didn't realise you actually wrote it.

Zakaria Of course.

Paul That's – great.

Zakaria I am writer.

Paul Yes.

Zakaria You are my reader.

Paul Zakaria, I can't read Arabic.

Zakaria This is not a problem.

Paul It is.

Zakaria I am your translator.

Paul Right.

Zakaria Sit, please.

Paul sits.

A boy lives in a village. His father makes mosaic. His mother has a very beautiful face. The boy tumbles in the grass. A boy is his friend. They walk along the highway. They ask, where is Damascus? Three girls sing. A man drives a car. In the sky there is an American. Two boys climb a tree to find America. A friend falls from a tree. He is dead. Three girls sing again. Now the boy is in the army. A bad thing happens. Now there is a dream. His friend is an eagle. They fly to America. Now the boy is awake. Now the boy is in Damascus. Now he is alone. He thinks of his mother's beautiful face. Now he dies. Three girls sing.

Paul Is that the end?

Zakaria This is the end.

This is my life.

You like it?

Paul I do.

Beat.

I like it. I genuinely like it.

It's beautiful.

Zakaria Yes.

Paul The boy and his friend.

Zakaria Yes.

Paul Beautiful.

Zakaria Yes.

Paul And sad.

Zakaria Yes.

Paul Very sad.

Zakaria Very sad.

Paul The boys climb a tree to find America.

Zakaria Yes.

Paul It's very true.

Zakaria It's my life.

I am a writer.

Paul Yes.
    Yes, you are.

    Beat.

Zakaria You propose my life in Hollywood.

Paul I really think Syrian TV might be a better –

Zakaria No, Mr Paul. Not Syrian TV. Syrian TV is not my life. I am in Hollywood. I am in Scotland, Mr Paul. Do you see Syrian TV? How to say this in English? I am not here, Mr Paul. I am not here one minute more.

Paul OK. OK. I understand.

Zakaria You propose me – in Hollywood?

Paul Yes. Of course. How old are you, Zakaria?

Zakaria I am twenty-three.

Paul Look – I'll . . . there might be schemes – bursaries – I'll see what I can do.

Zakaria You go back to Scotland with my life.

Paul Yes.

Zakaria OK.

Zakaria gives Paul the polythene bag full of papers.

Paul Thank you, Zakaria.

Zakaria Welcome.

THREE

The call to prayer begins.

The television shows news images of the current situation.

Elena On Friday afternoon it's empty, everyone's away at the mosque.
I play what I want.

Elena plays the finale of Olivier Messiaen's Turangalîla Symphony with full orchestral backing.

Applause, and Elena bows.

Thank you.

You're very kind.

FOUR

Muna enters from the street.
She sits.
She slams the 'Middleton Road' textbook down on the desk.

Wasim (*calling offstage*)
Thanks for the lift.
We'll see you next time we're in town
God willing.
You must come and visit the Institute.
It would be a privilege.
Goodbye, madam.
Goodbye.

> *Muna cringes at Wasim's obsequious goodbyes.*
> *Wasim enters.*

Well, I think we handled that very well.

Muna Do you?

Wasim You were amazing.
Really.
The way you stood up to her about janitorial
staffing levels.
'The environment in which our students learn is a
metaphor for the environment of the inside of their
heads. If their halls are untidy and carelessly looked
after, then so shall be their heads.'

Brilliant.

You had her.

Did you see her flinch?

And then when you started on about the need for new
multimedia equipment –

A firestorm.

> *Wasim catches Zakaria's eye.*

Two *café au lait*.

Muna I don't want coffee.

Wasim Darling, what's the matter?

Muna Don't touch me.

Wasim Apricot.

Muna 'What my colleague really means is . . .' 'Of
course, Minister . . .' 'Please, if I may intercede for a
moment to clarify . . .' 'My colleague is using heated
language, but what she really means is . . .' Every
point I made you softened.

Wasim It was a tactic, darling.

Muna You didn't let me say one word about the
textbook.

Wasim I was waiting for the right moment.

Muna Three times I tried to show it to her.

Wasim She was looking irritated.

Muna She said the President wanted to open the arms
of youth to the English-speaking world.

Wasim Did you see the way her eyes went to the clock?

Muna It was the perfect moment.

Wasim Why commit ourselves to one particular course
at this stage?

Muna Because she asked what we needed.

Wasim And we said – we said we needed more
contemporary work.

Muna We need this work.

Wasim It's one example, a good example of the sort
of work that we're looking for in order to effect the
President's aim of opening the arms of youth to –

Beat. Wasim speaks in a low voice.

Look, I wasn't going to tell you this, because it's not
necessarily . . . But word has it that the Minister might

be – she's in trouble. She's very much part of the old guard – she was a protégé of the President's father's. So the point is, the President needs space for new blood and she's . . . The exam results in the technical colleges have been poor again, and – she's nervous – you can see it in her eyes. She wouldn't take any risks just now. My advice – if you're determined to explore this particular . . . curriculum – is to wait until there's a new Minister. With luck he'll be of the more open tendency and – who knows what might happen?

Muna I felt ridiculous sitting there.

Wasim I have a feeling the new Minister will be more amenable.

Muna Drinking coffee. Chatting. Civilised.

Wasim That's why I wanted to bring you to the meeting. If you're going to be Dean yourself one day you'll need to learn to navigate –

Muna At one point I just looked at her.

Wasim – these waters that look calm but are in fact reefs.

Muna Her spectacles balanced on her nose like my old headmistress.

Wasim We went in with a certain amount of political capital. I think we've increased it. We've softened her up. All in all, it was a good meeting.

Muna It's just a textbook, Wasim, just a few words –

Wasim Exactly. Exactly. If it were a novel or a play –

Beat.

Muna What happened to you, Wasim?

Wasim Happened?

Muna When I was your student, you inspired me.

Wasim When you were my student it was my job to inspire you.

Muna You made everything seem possible.

Wasim When you're young everything does seem possible.

Muna No – those were harder times.

Wasim Youth makes the world seem boundless and changeable.

Muna We all adored you. You seemed so unafraid.

Wasim I was the campus Che Guevara. How much I loved the adoring stares of the girls. It's easy to be an inspiration to students when you're young and bright and you can offer them certainty. Muna, you know that. Tell them the world is changeable and that it's in their power to change it. They will fall in love with you. It's so easy, it's almost criminal. 'You have nothing to lose but your chains.' I almost believed it myself.

Muna You went to prison for it.

Wasim I went to prison to preserve my vanity, Muna.

Muna No. You went to prison for speaking the truth about the world.

Wasim Saying something over and over again does not make it the truth.

Beat.

Muna What do we offer the students now?

Wasim I'm not sure.

Muna They look around at the world and they need explanations. What do we tell them?

Wasim I'm not sure.

Muna When the fundamentalists tell them to dress in a certain way, what do we say?

Wasim I'm not sure.

Muna When the newspapers tell them their republic is a functioning democracy, what do we tell them?

Wasim I'm not sure.

Muna When the Americans tell them their government is evil, what do we say?

Wasim I'm not sure.

Muna Not sure. Not sure. It's cowardice. It's too easy.

Wasim Call it what you like, Muna, but it's not easy.

    Beat.

Doubt, hesitancy, timidity, uncertainty – these are the ways we go towards the truth. Slowly. Unsure of ourselves. 'Is this the right way?' 'Are you OK?' 'How is it for you?' And through the darkness we go. Slowly we walk forward putting out our hands to feel the damp walls of the cave. Looking for the light.

That is what we tell them.

Muna Do you remember the last time we were in Damascus?

Wasim Yes.

Muna We went up Mount Quissoon with Khaled and Aisha. You wore those ridiculous sunglasses. You and Khaled were dressed all in black. Aisha looked so beautiful. And you were all arguing and quoting.

Wasim I remember.

Muna I was nineteen. Out of my depth. Aisha talked

about patriarchy and Khaled about imperialism and you talked about orientalism.

Wasim Dear God, we must have bored you.

Muna No. No, you didn't. No, listening to you all it was as if the world suddenly swam into focus.

Wasim It was all pretentious . . . half-read . . . half –

Muna It was the most exciting thing I had ever heard.

Wasim Revolution.

Khaled works for a bank now. Aisha is a housewife in Dubai.

Muna You took me to a hotel. You said I was your wife.

Wasim I remember.

Muna We made love all afternoon. You refused to say you loved me because love was a bourgeois concept.

Wasim For that alone I deserved to go to prison.

Muna But I loved you.

Wasim I know.

Beat.

Wasim Let's go to Mount Quissoon.

Muna No.

Wasim It's still light. There's time.

Muna No.

Beat.

I said I would meet him here at seven.

Beat.

Wasim gets up to leave.

95

Where are you going?

Wasim I'm going to the mountain, darling, I'm going to take a look at the city.

Are you going to spend the night with him?

Muna I'm not sure.

Wasim leaves to the street.

Beat.

Muna leaves to the lift.

FIVE

Elena plays an arrangement of a song by a seventies singer-songwriter.

The television shows news images of the current situation.

Paul waits, paces, looks at his watch.

He makes a call on the hotel phone.

He puts the phone down.

He calls again.

Paul She's not answering.

She definitely went to her room?

Zakaria Yes.

Paul OK.

Zakaria I'm sorry.

Beat.

Elena Friday afternoons – seventies singer-songwriters. Cat Stevens, Jackson Browne. 'Blood on the Tracks' era Dylan. John Denver.

I admit it. John Denver is my weakness.

All right. All right. Calm down.

You really want to know what happened?

A boys' night out is what happened.

Paul Zakaria, I need a guide.

Zakaria I am your guide.

Paul You and me.

Zakaria I am your guide to the night.

Paul Let's go out. Let's find some girls.

Zakaria Of course.

SIX

Paul and Zakaria prepare for their night out.

Elena It was his last night alive and he spent it in debauch.

You don't want to know the details.

I'm telling you.

You won't like it.

Are you sure?

There are different reports. I pieced together a story.
There are some gaps. I may have to refer to my notes.

  Elena has some papers in a folder.

Paul Come on, Zakaria. Let's break up our lives.

Elena I always take notes.

I used to be KGB.

  Paul and Zakaria prepare to go out.

97

Zakaria changes his clothes. He combs his hair. He applies cologne.

Paul tries Muna on the phone one last time. He pours himself a beer. He waits for Zakaria.

Elena Receipt for a taxi to the Christian quarter at 8.00 p.m.

The driver says the Englishman pays twice the price. He leaves them at Bab Touma Gate where they continue on foot into the old city.

Receipts for twelve beers in The English Pub.

DJ that night was DJ Jack. DJ Jack says he sees an Englishman and Zakaria with two American girls. DJ Jack says that they talk and laugh for about two hours. Sometimes they dance. DJ Jack says his playlist that night is mostly Nirvana, REM and Michael Jackson.

Abdullah – the barman – says he hears an argument begin between the four of them at around 9.00 p.m. Zakaria becomes more heated and one of the American girls says:

'Fuck off. Fuck off, Zakaria. You're such a jerk.'

And the Englishman is heard to say:

'Come on, Zakaria. Come on. Come on, Kasey. Come on.'

Zakaria is heard to propose that they all four sleep together and one of the American girls is heard to say, 'No way, no fucking way.'

DJ Jack says that Zakaria dances alone to Queen's 'Crazy Little Thing Called Love'.

The American girl Kasey says she totally assumed that Zakaria was gay. Didn't he skip down the street? Didn't he actually skip at one point?

Abdullah says that at 10.00 p.m. Zakaria comes up to him and says he can't stand talking to the American girls any more and when Abdullah asks why, Zakaria says it's because they keep talking about suicide bombing and asking him if he is free to be all he can be. Zakaria says to Abdullah that he doesn't have the words in English to explain anything any more and it's pissing him off and does Abdullah know where he can buy any marijuana.

DJ Jack says that the Englishman and Kasey dance to Boney M's 'Nightflight to Venus'.

Abdullah says the Englishman seems drunk. He says the Englishman and Kasey dance to Arabic music. Paul makes eye-contact with Kasey. The Englishman puts his hand on Kasey's bottom.

At 10.55 p.m. DJ Jack says he overhears the Englishman invite the girls to the hotel for a foursome. He says, 'Seriously, ladies. I'm serious.'

At 11.00 p.m. the girls leave the pub.

At 11.05 Abdullah says he sees the Englishman begin crying.

At 11.07 Abdullah says he sees the Englishman gather himself.

At 11.10 Abdullah says he sees Zakaria and the Englishman staring into space – and Zakaria says:

'I am dead, Mr Paul. I am dead inside.'

At 12.00 p.m. a taxi receipt from Bab Sharki Gate back towards the hotel via Straight Street in the old city. The taxi driver says that as they drive through the narrow lanes and alleys the Englishman says:

'Fucking hell, it's like driving through the Bible.'

At 1.00 a.m. they are in the Café Aroma in New Damascus. They ask for beer. The café serves no beer.

The Englishman asks the proprietor where he can find some prostitutes.

At 1.30 a.m. Syria Tel report a phone call to a UK number:

NHS Direct?

I've lost my sense of smell.

'Do you have any other symptoms?'

No. I can smell piss.

'Have you noticed any other symptoms.'

No.

'It's probably viral. Give it time. It will come back of its own accord.'

Viral?

'Yes.'

Will I ever smell my children's hair again?

'You probably will.'

The smell of incipient rain?

'I expect so.'

Newly-mown grass?

'Almost certainly. Don't worry about it.'

Don't worry. That's easy for you to say. You still have all your faculties in full working order.

'Can I help you with anything else, sir?'

No. Thank you. Sorry.

At 1.30 a.m. a policeman reports hearing a young Arab man and an Englishman walk along Maysaloun Street singing:

'Maybe you're gonna be the one that saves me, but after all you're my wonderwall.'

At 1.45 a.m. they return to the hotel.

I was playing music.

It was early in the morning. I played the notes so far apart you could hardly tell it was music.

But it was.

SEVEN

Paul and Zakaria enter.

Elena plays the notes so far apart you can hardly tell that it's music.

Wasim watches television.

The television shows news images from the current situation.

Zakaria Fuck this place.

Paul Fuck America.

Zakaria Fuck you.

Paul Fuck Scotland.

Zakaria Fuck me.

Paul Fuck women.

Zakaria Fuck this country.

Paul Fuck Damascus.

Zakaria Fuck life.

Paul Fuck life!

Zakaria, we understand each other, you and I.

Zakaria Of course.

Paul We have a connection.

Zakaria We connect.

Paul We connect.

   Paul embraces Zakaria.

Thank you.

Zakaria Welcome.

Paul What time is it? Nearly two. I'm leaving in two hours.

It hardly seems worth going to sleep.

I'm going to stay up all night.

Zakaria You stay here with me.

Paul If I fall asleep now I'll never wake up.

Zakaria I will wake you.

Paul What about you? Will you stay awake?

Zakaria Of course.

Paul Thank you.

Zakaria embraces Paul.

Zakaria Wait. I get your suitcase. I bring it here.

Paul Everything's packed. It's just sitting on the bed.

Zakaria exits.

Wasim acknowledges Paul.

Dean.

Wasim Monsieur Paul.

Paul *Où est Muna?*

Wasim *Elle est dans sa chambre.*

Paul goes behind the bar. He takes a bottle of beer and opens it. He puts some money on the counter.

Paul *Bière?*

Wasim *Merci.*

Paul gives Wasim a beer.

He sits.

They both watch TV for a moment.

Paul *L'enfant. La petite fille. Sa visage.*

Wasim *Oui.*

Paul *C'est terrible.*

Wasim *Oui.*

Something of a pause.

Il y a autant des forces. Il y aura du sang.

Paul I'm sorry that's just – beyond –

Something of a pause.

Dean. I want to say. You and I – we maybe haven't
seen eye to eye. *Yeux a yeux. Mais, Monsieur le Dean –
merci. Merci pour votre invitation a Damascus* – because
if you hadn't invited me I wouldn't have seen the real
Damascus – *Damascus vrai – Et J'aime Damascus. J l'aime
beaucoup.*

Wasim toasts Damascus.

Wasim *A Damas.*

Paul *A Damas.*

Damas de la tête.

Wasim *Damas de la tête.*

The both toast again.

*L'année dernière j'étais à Dubai pour assister à un prix de
poésie –*

Paul Right. Dubai. Last year you were in Dubai for – a –

Wasim *– un prix de poésie.*

Paul A poetry prize.

Wasim *Et j'étais dans un hôtel sept étoiles.*

Paul Seven stars. That's a lot of stars. Poetry must be
very popular in Dubai.

Wasim *Un hôtel de luxe.*

Paul A de luxe hotel, *oui.*

> *Wasim takes out his phone.*
> *He shows Paul a photo on his phone.*

Wasim *Un hôtel de luxe.*

Paul This is the hotel.

Wasim *Partout des couloirs de miroirs.*

Paul Canyons full of mirrors.

Wasim *Partout des domestiques.*

Paul Cyclists? – Servants. Servants everywhere. It's – it's – God – it's amazing – for poetry.

Wasim *Un monde de luxe qui défie toute description.*

> *Paul doesn't understand.*

Un monde –

> *He shows Paul another photo.*

Paul This is the winner.

Not you.

Tu a gagné la prix?

Wasim Of course I didn't win the fucking prize. Some fucking rubbish about Palestine written by a Egyptian history teacher won the fucking prize.

Paul I'm sorry, I – Philistines? You were among Philistines?

Wasim They pay for us to stay in seven-star hotels. They give us prizes as long as we write about Palestine. But the moment we start writing about anything real – about . . . Oh, what's the point ?

Paul Really – my Arabic is non-existent.

Pardon.

Beat

Wasim There is a world
We do not see.
We do not speak.
We do not write.
This is my world.
Far away.

Zakaria enters with Paul's suitcase and his record player.

He also holds the polythene bag full of script.

Paul Oh, thank you, Zakaria.

Zakaria puts down the luggage.

Zakaria Mr Paul. I check the room. In case you forget something.

Paul Thanks.

Zakaria I find my life.

Paul What?

Zakaria Beside wastepaper basket.
With newspaper.
Also with guide to the mosque.

Zakaria shows Paul.

Paul Oh. I meant to . . . I – I just forgot to – you reminded me –

I'll just –

He takes the bag from Zakaria.

That was lucky.

Beat.

I'll take this back to Scotland and I'll –

Hollywood.

Zakaria I book taxi for you, Mr Paul.

Paul Thank you.

Zakaria Taxi come here.

Paul Right. If I fall asleep. You will wake me.

Zakaria Of course.

Paul Great.

Look – Zakaria, I hate goodbyes so –

I want you to have this.

   Paul offers Zakaria some dollars.

Zakaria No, Mr Paul.

Paul No, I insist.

Zakaria No.

Paul I insist, Zakaria.

Zakaria No.

Paul Really.

Zakaria No.

Paul Come on, Zakaria.

   Beat.

   Zakaria takes the money.

   Paul embraces Zakaria.

Thanks again for a great night out.

Sorry you didn't get a shag.

   Zakaria goes to reception.

   Paul doesn't quite know where to put the polythene bag.

   Paul looks at his suitcase. He looks at Zakaria's bag.

Dean, would you mind? Would you take a look at this for me?

Paul gives the Dean the plastic bag containing Zakaria's life.

Paul Is it – *les mots. C'est bon? Ou mal?*

Wasim looks through the script papers.

Wasim *Qui a écrit ca?*

Paul Zakaria.

Wasim *C'est ridicule. Ca n'a aucun rapport avec la réalité. C'est une fantasme.*

Paul Fantasy.
Right.

He gives the script back.

Paul OK. Thank you.

Wasim leaves to the lift.

Wasim *Bon voyage, Monsieur.*

Paul *Merci.*

Paul settles down to watch television.

Paul can't think what to do with bag. It won't fit in his suitcase.

Paul tries to pack the script away in his suitcase.

There is no room.

The bag breaks and papers fall out.

Paul Oh, for fuck's sake.

Paul tries to tidy up the papers.

The lift opens.
    Muna comes out.

It's late.

Muna I couldn't sleep.

Beat.

Paul Would you like a beer?

Muna No, thank you.
What's on TV?

Paul They're showing the child. Every hour, on the hour.
Crying for her father.

Muna The way she cries.

Paul It must be . . . The situation seems – what with the
Americans and the Israelis and what's happening in Gaza
and – it's getting worse.
But it's safe here.
No one would ever bomb Damascus.
Is that right?

Beat.

Paul sees the 'Middleton Road' book in her hand.

Were you reading?

Muna Yes.

Paul What were you reading?

Muna Conditional past tense.

Paul Jack and Nazeem.

Muna (*reads*) 'Jack, why were you walking on the
motorway?'
'Anything *could have* happened to you!'
'Nazeem – you *should have* called me.'
'*If you had* called me I *would have* come to fetch you
both.'

Paul Jack and Nazeem are picked up by the police.

108

Muna (*reads*)
    'We wanted to find the end of the city.'
    'If we had kept walking *would we have ever* found it?'

Paul The artist loved drawing that scene. The boys and the motorway.

Muna Very sweet.

Paul It's illegal, in Britain, to walk beside motorways.
    Here people walk wherever they want.
    Families have picnics by the side of the highway.
    There are no rules.

It really happened. My son and his friend. They just went off one day. He was only seven.

Muna You have a son?

Paul Yes. And a daughter.

Muna You didn't say.

    Beat.

Paul I rang the room, earlier, at seven.

Muna Yes.

Paul You must have been asleep.

    Beat.

We *could have* gone to the old city.

Muna I *could have* taken you to the mountain.

Paul That *would have* been nice.

    Muna smiles.

How did the meeting go with the Minister?

Muna It went well.

Paul Did you show her the book?

Muna It wasn't the right time.

Paul But you will . . .

Muna We can't take the book, Paul.

Paul Oh.

You wanted to make a stand.

Muna This doesn't just affect me. Not even just the Dean. If we make a stand, there will come a moment when my colleagues in the Institute will have to decide if they stand with me.

A few will.

Most won't.

The few who support me will do it out of duty. They will risk their position and future to back me and we will have no prospect of success. They will not thank me.

Those who feel unable to support me will add to their conscience another small defeat.

If it were a novel or a play . . .

Paul I see.

Muna I'm sorry.

Paul Don't be sorry.

   Beat.

Muna (*referring to the luggage*) You're going.

Paul Not for a few hours.

Muna You can sleep on the plane.

Paul Yes.

   Beat.

Look – I want you to have the record player. I can't be bothered lugging it all the way – you have it. A present.

Muna It's OK.

Paul I want you to have it and the music.

Muna No.

Paul For your brother.

Muna Paul. I have all the music I want on CD. I have iTunes. My brother is gone.

Paul Come up to my room.

Now.

    Beat.

Muna I'd better go.

Paul This morning, when we were dancing, you said something to me in Arabic. Whispered it.

Muna Yes.

Paul The words you used. *Love*, you said, something like *Love I love you my lover,* something like that.

Muna Yes.

Paul The words were in the song as well. *Lover lover.*

Muna Yes.

Paul What does it mean?

Muna Nothing.

    Paul Lover, lover I love you, lover.

What did you say?

    Muna Lover, you will never know you have been loved.

    Paul Love been never love . . .

    Muna Lover, you will never know you have been loved.

Paul Lover, you will never know you have been loved.

What does it mean?

Muna It's just a phrase.

Paul What does it mean?

Muna It means last night something happened.

Muna leaves to the lift.

Paul Lover never love lover –

I can't say it.

Muna leaves.

Beat.

Paul takes out his mobile.

Paul makes a call.

Paul It's me . . . Don't pick up – just to say I'm coming home. The snow melted and –

Well – plodding along.

I was in the market and I thought of you. Fruit and vegetables. The colours were amazing. Lemons and oranges and watermelons and . . . other indeterminate fruit. I thought of you.

You would like it here. You should come. We should bring the kids.

It's not a war zone.

It's not the way it's usually described.

It's . . . Oh, hi . . . Did I wake you? Sorry.

I thought you would have taken photographs of the piles of fruit in the market. I'd love to take you here some day – maybe one day we could both come and check in and spend a romantic, oriental Valentine's weekend . . . What are you thinking?

Wheel-bearings?

No I'm – I'm just – I don't have a tone.

I don't have a tone.

OK.

Night-night.

He ends the call.

Fuck. Piss. Cock.

Paul finds the record he played earlier.

He puts the record on the Dansette.

Paul (*to himself*) Lover never know you will be loved.

Paul makes himself comfortable on the chair.

Paul Lover never lover love.

He blows up his travel pillow.

He gathers up some of the script.

He looks at it.

Paul can't make any sense of the script.

He drops it on the floor.

Paul is falling asleep.

Zakaria enters.

He pours himself a whisky.

He drinks.

Zakaria Mr Paul.

Paul Mmm?

Zakaria Those girls are very beautiful.

Paul I'm tired, Zakaria.

Zakaria Josephine is very beautiful

Paul Mmm.

Zakaria Josephine is in Valence.

Paul Mmm.

Zakaria For a visa I must have invitations. Every year I apply for a visa. Every year the visa is not approved.

Everyone is in the village, in my father's house, all their wives, all their children. Many, many children. Everybody sits around the big table. I am here. I am in Damascus.

Paul is asleep.

Zakaria gathers up the script.

He puts the script back in the bag.

He takes out a gun from out of his pocket.

Elena The gun was made in Russia and sold to Iraq. It was an Iraqi army standard issue officer's revolver. After the invasion the Baghdad armoury was looted by an opportunistic quartermaster who sold the guns to a new insurgent militia. An ex-civil servant from the oil ministry was issued with it and used it to shoot at American trucks. As the situation deteriorated, the civil servant sold up and took his family across the border. He put the gun in a secret compartment under the driver's seat. When he got to Damascus he sold the gun to a young man associated with the Islamic Brotherhood who had decided to take up *jihad*. But the young man got a place in a technical college in Egypt and his parents arranged a marriage to a girl he quite liked so he decided to abandon *jihad* and he sold the gun on to a dealer who hung around the mosque. The dealer sold it to Kamal, who was thinking of going to Chechnya. One night, when

they were talking in Kamal's damp room in the old city, Zakaria saw the gun and he asked Kamal if he could borrow it. Just for a while. Just in case.

Zakaria points the gun at Paul.

Kamal said yes.

A taxi horn sounds.
It sounds again.

Mr Paul.

Paul Mmm.

Zakaria Taxi is here.

Wake up, Mr Paul.
Wake up.

Paul Mmm.

Zakaria puts the gun to himself.

A moment.

Zakaria shoots himself.

Zakaria?

Paul goes to Zakaria.

Paul holds Zakaria's hand as he dies.

You twat.

Zakaria.

EIGHT

Elena I remember the smell.

Blood and whisky.

Do you remember that smell?

Poor Zakaria.

Shit happens.

Elena shuts the piano.

What else do you want me to say?

What else could a transsexual Ukrainian Christian Marxist cocktail pianist possibly say that would make things any better for you?

You held his hand.

When he died he was not alone.

You held his hand.

I know.

I was here.

I'm always here.

The End.